# *One Hope at a Time:*
## THE PRISONER OF
# HOPE
## LETTERS
### BOOK TWO

---

Robyn Franceen Evans

2 | *The Prisoner of Hope Letters*

Copyright © September 2017 by Robyn Franceen Evans
One Hope at a Time: The Prisoner of Hope Letters, Book Two

All rights reserved. No part of this book may be reproduced or transmitted in any form or by any means without written permission from the author.

ISBN: 978-1974224524


Printed in the United States of America
Robyn Franceen Evans, Publisher
www.butterflysister.com
hellobutterflysister@gmail.com

Cover art and graphics by GalanGraphix.com
Author photo by Shelley C. Sterrett

## Dedication

For my godchildren—in your faces I see the insight of hope and the promise of greater days. May each one of you become unshakable in your belief and trust of the triune God. Your names are written across my heart.

For my son—your loving acceptance gives me hope every day. I thank God for the man you are and the man you are becoming. There is no step between us, only love.

For every person that helps my mom—your actions keep my hope vibrant and new.

## Preface

I am thankful to witness this season of life, even though it comes with many challenges. Look around you. The world continues to change just as the Lord said it would. What's encouraging about that? His people are changing, too. One by one, we are emerging from the shadows of selfishness and into the light of purpose.

Father God has called us to do great things. What a joy to see His children begin to grasp His plan! I am just one of many believers who have begun to step into the light of purpose. For so many years I ignored that still, small voice encouraging me to write. I ignored it until it began to scream. I was so focused on my perceived inadequacy and paralyzed by my brand of perfection that I was missing one of the greatest joys I have ever known—receiving messages from readers who were blessed by the words God gave me.

As I continue to grow into the writer He called me to be, I am humbled by the awesomeness of this journey. I am honored that He gave me the ability to express the visions in my mind and I pray that you will connect with at least one letter in this book in a supernatural way.

We often speak of needing a breakthrough. It is my hope that the words in this book will usher you into the freedom you have longed for.

If you purchased my first book in this series, you will notice a few changes in this second book. First, I am encouraging you in this book to pick up your Bible. I have provided scripture references for you to look up on your own. This way, you can choose to read from your favorite translation. Also, I am asking a question at the end of each letter in hopes that you will earnestly take time to answer it. I have provided a small space in the back of this book for your thoughts, but I highly encourage the purchase of a journal. It does not have to be fancy, but it is a great way to get all of your thoughts on paper and look them over.

I know that picking up your Bible will bless your life. I am sure that writing your thoughts down will focus your life. I am praying that this book will help you to see hope in Jesus on a whole new scale and commit your ways to Him wholeheartedly.

"See" you in book three!

# The Prisoner of Hope Letters

# Letter 1
# Show Mercy

*Please read Matthew 5:7.*

January 7, 2013

Dear soul,

One of my favorite movies is *The Karate Kid*, starring Ralph Macchio. It's about a young boy who comes of age after he moves to a new town. Not long after arriving, he gets picked on by the local bullies and decides that he must find a way to defend himself.

He sees a karate dojo in town and thinks about learning martial arts to defend himself, but the same kids who are picking on him are already in the class. As they train, they repeat the phrase: "Strike first. Strike hard. No mercy."

In Japanese, dojo means "place of the way." The leader of a dojo is known as a sensei, which literally means "person born before another." In other words, a sensei should be wise because he or she is teaching the next generation.

Can you imagine what kind of generation is born from a merciless mindset? There are many today who have adopted such a mindset. They want mercy for themselves, but are unwilling to dispense it to others.

Jesus said that those who show mercy are truly blessed. In their time of need, they will be shown mercy.

You may be in a situation right now where you need mercy. If not, the time will come. Pour mercy upon people every chance you get, it's like spring rain. Pray first. Pray hard. Show mercy.

> **Journal:** What does mercy mean to you? When have you needed mercy the most? Have you ever extended mercy?

# Letter 2
# Real Treasure

*Please read Matthew 6:19-21.*

January 14, 2013

Dear soul,

I'm in a reflective mood.

I've been thinking about who I am, what I've done and what I have. That old familiar tape began to play. You know the one. I should be better, I should have done better and I should have more...

We can all use a little improvement, but often not in the areas we think.

I kept focusing on some things I long for, but don't have. I don't have my own home with the in-home game/theater room. I don't have a large home office. I don't have thousands of dollars in the bank, or an investment portfolio.

Jesus didn't have those things either, but He *is* wealth.

It's not that there's anything wrong with desiring such things or working to get them, but we must remember the temporary nature of it all. Our true home doesn't have earthly walls. We should never be so wrapped up in earth that we forget that it is only a fraction of our existence.

So, if you don't get your LCD TV down here, remember that you'll have an eternity to watch the handiwork of God—in beyond high definition!

Build your home in heaven and let it be the focus of your heart. No bank will ever be able to take it away from you.

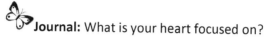
**Journal:** What is your heart focused on?

# Letter 3
# Hope for More

*Please read Romans 8:24.*
January 21, 2013

Dear soul,

You can't hope for what you already have. If you have everything, why would you need hope?

When hope is absent, we malfunction. We are born with a desire for more. As we grow, we learn just what "more" really is.

More is the promise of a future without earthly boundaries. It's the absence of pain, death and taxes. More is not having to say goodbye to loved ones. More is grasping the source of joy, unspeakable. More is the truest form of wealth—the rest of God.

If every need was met by earthly provisions, why would we ever need a savior? What would be the purpose of Heaven? We all need something to look forward to just as a young child waits for Christmas Day. Hope pulls a thread of excitement through our lives. It's not some cosmic dangling carrot, but a real state of security. When God wraps a gift, it is perfect and perfectly delivered to all who vow to never lose hope.

> **Journal:** What is your greatest hope?

# Letter 4
# God is...

*Please read Psalm 28:7.*
January 28, 2013

Dear soul,

God is.

On Saturday night, the song, *God Is*, came into my spirit. I haven't heard it in a while, but it was so on time for me. I love how God sends you little whispers of His love and care. I love that my God is not some inanimate object or lofty figure of doom. He is just, but He is also merciful and full of love. True love.

The next morning, I visited a church with my Michael and not too long after we got there, the choir stood to sing a song. As I heard the beginning chords of the song, I grabbed his arm and said, "Honey, this is the song I shared with you yesterday!" He just smiled and said, "I know. Isn't God awesome?"

I lifted my hands in praise as they sang. I was so overwhelmed by God's love for me. I rocked back and forth and closed my eyes.

When I opened my eyes, there was a single phrase on the projector screen in the front of the church: God is.

Our hope is not in a feeling or a song, for they are merely manifestations of our response to Him! Our hope is rooted in the only One who can keep us from falling and present us blameless. I don't care how much we try to stay clean and on the straight and narrow, Father God sees us through the finished work of His son, Jesus.

Yes, we strive for the mark, but Jesus has already won the race (and He did it with all of us hanging onto Him as He crossed the finish line)! Our weight didn't slow Him down, it just made Him stronger.

Cast your weights upon him. He cares and He is!

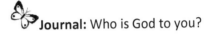**Journal:** Who is God to you?

# Letter 5
# The Royal Family

*Please read Matthew 3:17.*
February 4, 2013

Dear soul,

Look at what Father God did for His Son. When you accept Jesus as your Lord and Savior, Father God sees you through the redeeming sacrifice of His Son.

In short, He is pleased with you and calls you His own. Remember that the next time you feel rejected, dismissed or unimportant.

This world has a way of trying to strip you of the royalty you've inherited through Christ.

I'm just here to remind you of who you really are—a child of the King!

> **Journal:** Meditate on your royal lineage. How does it feel to be a child of the KING?

# Letter 6
# Life Verse

*Please read Philippians 4:6.*
February 11, 2013

Dear soul,

In my opinion, every child of God should have at least one life verse. A life verse is a verse or bank of scriptures that you closely relate to. It is a message to your soul to keep you focused and grounded in Christ.

Anyone who knows me, knows that Matthew 6:33 is my main life verse. It reminds me to keep God as the object of my pursuits in this life. He reminds me that if I live that way, He will take care of everything I need.

I've just added a second life verse, Philippians 4:6. For the past year, this verse has appeared repeatedly in my life and most notably as I started 2013. When God repeats anything, pay extra attention.

I like the way God deconstructs and reconstructs us. When we ask Him to search us, He will. When we ask Him to cast out anything that is not like Him, He does. God kept putting in my spirit that I was anxious and He was not pleased. He reminded me that there is nothing wrong with asking, as long as I am asking Him.

When I ask myself or others to supply my needs, the same thing always happens. We fall short. After the fall, we feel anxious. We wonder why it didn't work or why we are so stressed. We don't understand why it won't just come together perfectly.

Man will never create a perfect anything, but God is the author of perfection. Let your request be made known to Father God, seek Him first in all you do and you will have the very best Heaven has to offer. Take your eyes off of what you think you want or need and leave Him room to amaze you with what you could never dream up for yourself! Anxious? No. Hopeful? Yes!

> **Journal:** Do you have a life verse? Why or why not?

# Letter 7
# Never, Ever Alone

*Please read Deuteronomy 31:8.*
February 18, 2013

Dear soul,

Recently, a man shared that he was through with God.

Have you ever been there? It sounds like a scary place to be, doesn't it? It's hard to imagine being through with the one who created us. Without Him, we would not exist.

We all go through seasons in life much like the seasons we experience in our atmosphere. There is a time of winter and the barren feeling seems unending. There is a time of spring, where there is a revival of the spirit and everything feels fresh, new and green. The heat of the summer burns off excess junk, and in the fall we shed the old to make room for the new.

Are you angry with God? Tell Him how you feel. He can handle it. Feeling like life is unfair? You can tell Him about that, too. Feel like you can't talk to Him anymore? Ask someone else in the faith to intercede for you.

Just remember that this journey is not for the faint of heart. As a child of God, you have everything you need to emerge victorious. Don't mistake a difficult season for God's abandonment. His Word is true. He's not through with us.

> **Journal:** Have you ever been angry with God?

# Letter 8
# Rescue Me!

*Please read Luke 22:44.*
February 25, 2013

Dear soul,

Have you ever prayed in a state of anguish? If you have, you know that your prayers are more direct and sincere. It's not the gratuitous "now I lay me down," it's more like the "rescue me!" When we stand in need of help, we don't play around.

I want you to see a portrait of Christ as He prepared to go to the cross. He had already been through several savage beatings, unjust trials and public humiliation, yet He still pressed toward the cross.

One of the reasons I love Jesus so much is because He really knows me.

He is not some out of touch figure on high that dares me to get close to Him. He knows my sorrow, but more than that, He knows my hope for tomorrow. What seemed like an end on the cross was a beginning for us and a triumph for good. Evil tries its best to stamp out good, but good keeps coming out on top.

When you pray today, imagine being next to Jesus in Gethsemane. Speak from your heart with full assurance that He is listening. The only One who was crucified in anguish, was resurrected in hope.

**Journal:** Write down a prayer for today.

# Letter 9
# The Doctor is in!

*Please read Matthew 9:9-13.*

*This was written with my husband, Michael.*

March 4, 2013

Dear soul,

We need a doctor that is above all doctors. Jesus loves all people but has come to call outcasts. You see, when Jesus changes any man, that man will change everybody around him.

There is no way you can come in contact with Jesus and be the same. I feel like he definitely reaches out to everyone, but has a special ministry toward so-called social outcasts. Back in the day, tax collectors were considered the lowest of the low but that didn't stop him from going to Zacchaeus' home.

No matter what problems anyone has or will go through, Jesus will cover it all. It doesn't matter if society accepts or rejects you. His arms are open. Even if no one understands or loves you, Jesus never stops loving you, no matter who you are and regardless of what you've done!

Jesus is a healer and fixes broken people. We are all broken in some way and need his healing and help. When people are in pain and are enduring suffering, they go to a doctor for healing. So, no matter what is on your mind and whatever you are going through, give it to the doctor above all doctors.

That is a prescription for hope, signed with the blood of Jesus—and you can understand the writing on the slip!

**Journal:** If you could write a prescription for hope, what would it include?

# Letter 10
# Big Plans

***Please read Jeremiah 29:11.***
March 11, 2013

Dear soul,

I got rocked last night. Been there? I mean everything is going along just fine and boom! You get news you just weren't ready for. Are you ever ready for news that flips your equilibrium?

I know I'm not.

But here is the beautiful part about last night: It only took me about 30 minutes to recover. That's a victory for me. You know why I recovered so quickly? I went to Father God in prayer.

I'm growing!

I stepped away from everyone and looked up at the stars. I felt peace in His presence. I told Him what was on my heart and asked Him to guide me. He gave me Jeremiah 29:11.

It doesn't matter what curve balls man throws my way or what plot the enemy is cooking up. God has great plans for me. The closer I get to this truth, the less I can be moved. I am keenly aware, more than ever, that this world is temporary. Every pain I feel is temporary, because I am His child and I haven't even begun to live. I am eternal. This helps me keep everything in perspective.

What about you, dear soul? Did you get news that turned you upside down? Are you hurting? Whatever you are going through, just remember that it won't last. I don't know about you, but that gives me hope and a desire to fight on to the end, which will be my beginning. Hope on.

**Journal Prompt:** Name three things you believe God will manifest in your life.

## Letter 11
## Chief Intercessor

*Please read Romans 8:25-27.*

March 18, 2013

Dear soul,

Sometimes it's hard to keep our composure when we are waiting—especially if we've waited for a long time.

That's why I am glad we have help along this journey. The Holy Spirit was sent to help us. He helps us to stay composed and communicates on a level we cannot verbalize. He knows what we desire. He knows what we need. Even though we can't put it together properly, He gets it.

If we moan, He understands it. If we groan, He comprehends it. He fixes our request and takes it to the Father on our behalf.

Whatever you stand in need of and hope for, just know that God hears you, and in due time it shall be released to you in harmony with His perfect will. Don't be disappointed if it shows up differently than you requested. God isn't into order fulfillment. He specializes in upgrades.

> **Journal:** Write a letter to God about a request you made that has not happened.

# Letter 12
# Pursue Wisdom

*Please read Proverbs 2:3-5.*
March 25, 2013

Dear soul,

I've been reading the book of Proverbs all month long because I am seeking wisdom.

When I read this verse, it made me think of a time when I thought I'd lost something of great value. I could not sleep. I spent every moment possible looking for my treasure. I relentlessly sought after my treasure. It took several hours before I found my treasure, but when I found it the time didn't matter at all. I was so thankful, excited and relieved that I found it, that I would have started the search all over again just to relive that moment of joy.

This is the way we should be with seeking the wisdom of God. Relentless. This is how we should hope: relentlessly.

**Journal:** What are you seeking today?

# Letter 13
# We Rise!

*Please read Matthew 28:6.*
April 1, 2013

Dear soul,

God never speaks idle words. Whatever He speaks comes to pass. He spoke mountains and they formed. He spoke light and it flourished. He speaks and it is so. He speaks and it is finished. He speaks and it begins.

My joy is full and overflowing today because in a world of endless chatter, I have peace in the Word. He said He would rise, and He did. With his ascent, we also rise.

He is risen!

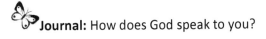
**Journal:** How does God speak to you?

## Letter 14
## Let Us Go

*Please read John 11:44.*
April 8, 2013

Dear soul,

Lazarus was dead.

He'd been dead for four days. He was indisputably dead. He was buried in a low place. Down a flight of 24 jagged rock steps, through a small room and down another small flight of steps, his body laid. He was covered in death wraps, much like a mummy.

When you are dead, there is no thought for the mobility of the body.

Jesus, even in the midst of performing miracles, shows a servant's heart and invites us to be a part of the miracle. He could have stood alone, a four day's journey away from the tomb and spoke life into Lazarus, but he made the journey. He could have stood at the top of the steps to the tomb and called forth Lazarus, but it is believed that he descended down those 24 steps before he spoke to his friend. He could have spoken to the stone that covered Lazarus' tomb, but he invited those around him to remove it themselves. Can you imagine the stench of that enclosed space? In the darkness of a cave, Jesus spoke forth life.

Lazarus emerged, still wrapped in the remnants of death. He struggled to walk because he was bound so tightly, but yet he emerged free from the grip of death. Jesus could have spoken those death wraps off of him, but he invited those around him to remove the grave clothes.

There is a bit of Lazarus in each of us. We wrap ourselves in things that steal our lives away. Jesus is willing to come from above to go down into the deep places in our lives and call us out of death. He puts people around us to help us receive our miracle and He invites us to take part in the miracle we've asked for.

He could have floated Lazarus out of the tomb, but He let him walk. Keep walking, dear soul. Let your loved ones help you get out of your grave clothes. The living have no need for grave clothes. Leave worthless attire alone and choose to be wrapped in the richness of hope that was fulfilled more than 2000 years ago by Jesus Christ, who is still calling forth the dead, even now.

Come forth!

> **Journal:** What are you spiritually wrapped in that must come off? Anger? Bitterness? Defeat?

## Letter 15
## Content

*Please read Philippians 4:11.*
April 15, 2013

Dear soul,

Paul arrived at a place in life where he was content. What a great place to be! Do you realize how much stress we heap upon ourselves when we cease to be content with what we have?

Being content doesn't mean you have resigned to the possibility of having more and doing more. It means that you will be grateful for your current state in this world. It means that you will focus on where you are right now and resolve to bloom whether in the desert or a beautiful garden.

You don't get there by theories. You get there by learning. Strive to learn what God is teaching you right now and be grateful for the lessons. Perhaps that's the key to moving beyond where you are right now.

Be content. Be teachable. Be ready to move when God speaks.

> **Journal:** What do you believe God is trying to teach you right now?

# Letter 16
# Lively Hope!

*Please read I Peter 1:3.*
April 22, 2013

Dear soul,

Have you ever considered God's relationship with himself? He is three persons, yet He is one. He has fellowship with himself. That really blows my mind. Even though He already had himself for fellowship, and a creation to enjoy, He still made us. He still wanted us.

Yes, wayward-meaning-well-trouble-making us.

I can meditate on that indefinitely. It makes me feel so valuable and needed. But to know that He made us even though He knew we'd betray Him just shows me the vastest expanse of love I could ever imagine. He knew what we would do and still made a costly provision to bring us back to His side. He gave Himself when we were at our worst.

Through the resurrection of His son, we are given a lively hope. We are brought back into a state of Eden where we can walk and talk with Him as if we'd never left His side.

Lively hope—that's the only kind I need!

> **Journal:** Imagine you are in Eden having a conversation with God. What would you talk about?

## Letter 17
## Answered Prayers

*Please read Matthew 6:33.*
April 29, 2013

Dear soul,

This is my life verse. I believe everyone should have one. It's a verse that keeps you sane in a crazy world. It's a voice that stills the boat when the seas get rough. It's an anchor and a compass. I adopted it more than a decade ago. Every time I would get anxious, confused or sad about my place in life, I'd refer to it for clarity. It always brings me back to a place of calm. It reminds me that God will take care of every need I have.

All I have to do is seek Him before the need.

Seeking Him opens the windows of Heaven. Seeking Him lets Him know that no matter what your need is, you need Him above all. I sit here today filled with awe as I think about the events of the last decade. This weekend, God showed me why it pays to wait on Him. I saw five prayers answered in less than 48 hours.

Prayer #1: Lord, please send me a spiritual man who loves your Word.

Results: I woke up excited on my birthday! My first text message was from Michael, the love of my life. He wrote me a beautiful spiritual vitamin about God's love that referenced I Corinthians 13.

Prayer #2: Lord, please send me a man who listens to my needs and responds to them.

Results: My shoulders are really tight and I am under a great deal of stress right now. Michael paid attention to that, and for my birthday, sent me to get a full body, deep tissue, hot stone treatment massage. Later, he took me to my favorite restaurant. He listens to me and knows what I like, what I need and what I want.

Prayer #3: Lord, I'd like to receive three dozen red roses one day from someone who loves me.

Results: Michael sent me exactly three dozen red roses.

Prayer #4: Lord, I'd like to know what it feels like to have my man throw me a birthday party and cook for me.

Results: Michael organized a beautiful birthday party, he cooked for me (yum!!) and I even got a super yummy cake with my picture on it!

Prayer #5: Lord, send me a man who loves you more than he loves me and wants to spend the rest of his life with me.

Results: On my birthday, surrounded by our families, Michael wrote 36 reasons why I am the woman for him. I read each one out loud, crying through them...then he got down on one knee and asked me to marry him. I said yes with my mouth as well as my heart!

These things did not happen because I am so great. My prayers were not answered because I never do anything wrong. These things happened because God is awesome, and He rewards those who diligently seek him. God knows what I need and the desires of my heart. When I decided to seek Him first, my life perspective changed. When my perspective changed, it set a chain reaction in motion that took eight years to reach me.

Eight years before God sent Michael to me, I prayed that God would give me the patience and grace to wait on the man He wanted me to marry. I was content with not dating because I knew what I wanted. It was a long eight years, but when I looked into Michael's eyes as he asked me to marry him, I knew I'd wait another eight years just to experience that moment all over again.

Whatever you are waiting for, and whatever you need, remember that God can and will supply all of your needs, and throw in some of your desires, too. Continue to hope for what only God can bring to pass. I am a living witness that He will add everything you need into your life at just the right time.

Stand upon Him, for He is hope fulfilled. All other ground is sinking sand.

> **Journal:** Thank God for what you are hoping for as if you already have it.

# Letter 18
# LOVE

*Please read I Corinthians 13.*
May 6, 2013

Dear soul,

Love endures and conquers all things. The ultimate sacrifice by God was His greatest act of love for us, so no matter how much we love each other, God loves us more.

Love conquers hate and endures pain, that's why people search, hope and yearn for it in life—because of its healing power.

We can change the world, one person at a time by putting a little more love in our hearts every day.

We look for and want love from a man or woman, but the greatest love story of your life will always be your relationship with God. There is no higher love or feeling so seek God first and at all times.

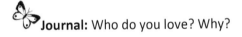
**Journal:** Who do you love? Why?

## Letter 19
## Get in!

*Please read Luke 8:22.*
May 13, 2013

Dear soul,

Even though the sun always shines, it will not always shine on you. Clouds come. Winds blow. Storms brew. It's natural.

It's supernatural to be calm in the midst of turmoil. Jesus' disciples, based on His words, got into a boat. They knew nothing of the journey before them, but they had enough faith to get into the boat.

I think it takes great faith to get into a boat. Think about it. You are at the mercy of the surrounding water. The farther you go out the more vulnerable you are. At some point, you won't be able to swim back to shore once you leave the safety of shallow water.

No matter what you are going through, if you trust in Jesus He will take you to the other side. You may arrive with a few scars, but He has those too. In fact, when you see him face to face, He'll still be wearing those scars, reminding you that He will always take you to the other side.

Get in the boat. Set out.

> **Journal:** Are you ready to get out of the boat? What do you need to take your first step?

# Letter 20
# Spirit of Hope

*Please read I Corinthians 2:14.*
May 20, 2013

Dear soul,

Spirit recognizes spirit. Flesh recognizes flesh. Spirit and flesh cannot speak the same language.

The Spirit is well acquainted with hope. Such hope is alive, backed up by the Word of God and as sturdy as the main cornerstone of a building. It is not a flimsy hope filled with the wishes of man.

When you say that you hope in the spirit realm, you are waiting with expectancy for something God-breathed to come to pass. Fleshly hope has no such guarantee. Fleshly hope deals in chance, spins wheels and rolls dice.

If you share what you are hoping for in the spirit with someone who is not acquainted with the Spirit of God, you cannot expect them to believe or know what you are talking about. In fact, they may laugh at you.

The laughter will be silenced. I am a witness. When God turns your hope into a reality, the laughter will cease. God can use your testimony of hope fulfilled to show the flesh what real hope looks like...and it's a beautiful sight to see flesh bow to the Spirit. Stay expectant.

> **Journal:** Make a list of at least 20 things you are hoping to receive.

## Letter 21
## Destiny

*Please read Genesis 30:22.*
May 27, 2013

Dear soul,

You are not forgotten.

Whatever you must give birth to will come. You may feel as though God has forgotten you, but your name is written across His heart.

Rachel was not forgotten.

When God remembers you, it isn't a discovery. He's always known you. He knew you before your parents. When He remembers you, it's a breakthrough. It's because the appointed time has come for you to be showcased in a way that only He can direct.

He touches dead situations and brings life. He breathes on impossible odds.

Your hope keeps you at the forefront of His thoughts. It lets Him know that you will trust Him even when it feels fruitless.

Feelings and truth don't always match. Cling to this truth: He remembers you.

Your day will come. In fact, it may already be here. You may just need new eyes to see.

---

**Journal:** Write a letter to thank God for remembering you.

## Letter 22
## Take Me to the Water

*Please read Romans 8:13.*

June 3, 2013

Dear soul,

Have you ever seen a shark out of water? It's not so tough when it's outside of its natural habitat. It can no longer be feared because the medium of strength that empowers the shark to be everything it was intended to be...is gone.

Have you ever seen a Christian functioning outside of the Spirit?

Scary.

No matter how many rows of teeth a shark has, how fast it can swim, or how powerful of a bite it can exhibit, those things are rendered useless when water is absent.

The Spirit will not leave. He cannot be drained or evaporated like water. When you received the Spirit, He was sealed into you with supernatural power. He gives you strength to accomplish any and every task set before you. The same resurrecting power that raised Jesus from the dead is housed in your body and surrounded by flesh.

Since flesh is merely our physical clothing, why do we give it homage above our cloak of righteousness? Operating in the flesh is like being a shark on land.

No power.

Think of the Spirit as water. When you are immersed, you are unstoppable. And anyone who tries to attack you, must come on your turf. That includes enemies who masquerade as fierce wolves. The most ferocious wolf is no match for a shark who is in its proper environment.

All that you hope for is present. Each fulfilled hope hangs in the heavens. Only through the Spirit will you be able to reach them.

Stay in the water.

> **Journal:** Are you in the right environment?

# Letter 23
# Unlocked

*Please read Ephesians 5:18.*
June 10, 2013

Dear soul,

Yesterday my pastor preached about the Holy Spirit and I was convicted. You see, I don't pay enough attention to the Spirit. If I did, my life would be vastly different.

The Spirit doesn't make life easy, but He makes life livable, conquerable and peaceful in ways we can never comprehend. We only need call upon Him and ask Him for help in any tough thing we are facing, so why do we tighten our lips and refuse to ask?

We fill ourselves with so many things that tear us down. We fill ourselves with anxiety, fear, doubt, and depression. Then we try to use stuff to fix what we are filled with such as food, drugs, alcohol, and entertainment.

We are stuffed, but we are not fixed. We are fat, but we are not full.

We find temporary comfort, but why? Why, when we know the only filling that can take us through the struggles of this life is just waiting to expand in our souls? The Spirit longs to be called upon daily. He will give you freshness every day. Just ask.

My pastor asked why we often lock ourselves up in bad emotions and throw away the key. I don't know why we do it, but I hope we stop doing it for our own good. Just remember that no matter where you throw that key, it is within the Spirit's grasp.

Ask Him to unlock you today and experience what a Spirit-filled life looks like.

> **Journal:** What did you use as temporary comfort in the past? What about now?

## Letter 24
## When Jesus Comes

*Please read I Thessalonians 4:16.*
June 17, 2013

Dear soul,

Recently I was blessed to visit my youngest nephew's first-grade classroom. His teacher had organized a wonderful author event for the young writers. Each student published one book. They worked so hard! They wrote the story and illustrated each page. They were so proud and it was clear to me just how much they needed encouragement and support by watching their body language.

Not just anyone's support would do. They were looking for validation from their parents. They squirmed in their seats and kept watching the entrance of the room. As the teacher gave instructions, they tried to listen, but each time a parent arrived a mixture of joy and sighs filled the room. It was an atmosphere of great expectation, but it was also frustrating for the children whose parents did not come.

As I watched the children, I could not help of think of Jesus' return. I think of how his followers stared at the sky long after He'd ascended into heaven. I think of how, even though we have instructions to follow and a purpose to fulfill, we cannot help but stare at the sky ourselves wondering when He will return.

In truth, we are like the books each child worked on. With each day we write the pages and illustrate them through our choices. We look for validation.

"Lord, do you see me?"

"I colored in the lines this time, Father."

"Holy Spirit, thank you for helping me finish this paragraph. It's been a long day!"

As we live, the volumes increase. As we grow, we become more concise. We begin to concern ourselves less with time because we realize it is short. Instead, we concentrate on moving forward.

As I get older, I am less concerned about WHEN Jesus will return. Rather, I am consumed by the fact that He WILL. Because I know He will, even though I look at the clouds in anticipation, I am happy to stay focused on what He called me to do while I am still here.

Hope is expected fulfillment and Jesus is our hope. Keep watching the sky, but don't let that stop you from your calling. We are not called to gaze, but to amaze.

**Journal:** What has Jesus called YOU to do?

## Letter 25
## Open the Door

***Please read Luke 19.***

June 24, 2013

Dear soul,

I think everyone has had at least one competitive moment in life. A lonely wife may compete with her husband's love affair with sports. She just wants to be seen and heard. A despondent husband may compete with his wife's group of besties. He just wants to be respected and honored. A seasoned professional may compete with an entry-level phenom for a spot on a coveted project...

No matter what you are going through in life, you will experience competitive moments from time to time. Aren't you glad God doesn't make you compete for his attention? When all else fails (and it will), the triune God is your constant audience.

He sees you. He knows you. He loves you.

Zacchaeus may have been short in stature, but he was a giant in the eyes of Christ Jesus. He put forth great effort just to see the Master, but Jesus saw him before the foundations of the world. Jesus saw his heart and sought after him. He made a special trip to his home to fellowship with him.

When you are frustrated and feel like no one understands or sees you, think of Zacchaeus and put yourself in his shoes. Read the scripture and put your name in the account.

Get out of the tree and get ready to receive the blessings of Jesus. He may already be at your house waiting for you to let Him in.

Open the door to hope.

> **Journal:** Are there times in life when you feel you are in a competition? If so, when?

# Letter 26
# Declaration of Dependence

*Please read John 15:5.*
July 1, 2013

Dear soul,

As we look ahead to July 4, also known as Independence Day, I can't help but think of the state of the nation. As we celebrate our nation's independence, it pains me to see how far we've come from where we started. We started with God, but it seems that we are determined to end without Him.

Perhaps we should create a Declaration of Dependence.

Perhaps we need to be reminded that our power is in our connection with Him, not our separation.

We shake our fists in the face of God and tell Him that He is not wanted in our schools, homes, bedrooms—and even in some churches. We may not say it outright, but actions are the megaphone of the soul.

In these perilous times, stay connected to the only One who is able to keep you from falling and present you to the Father with great joy. Stay connected to the vine.

> **Journal:** Write your own declaration of dependence on Jesus Christ.

## Letter 27
## Where are You?

**Please read Ephesians 4:26.**
July 15, 2013

Dear soul,

As I walk along this journey, one of my hopes is that I am improving over time. Last night I encountered a situation that tested where I am.

I have a long way to go.

I was at a drugstore with my Michael. He was happily reading something and I was searching for cold drinks. It was hot outside. The kind of hot you can feel. You know it's hot when you feel the sweat running down your back under your shirt and the rest of your clothes are sticking to you.

I pulled open a glass door and picked a few ice cold beverages. All was well. I went to the register to pay. The cashier greeted me warmly and I returned the reply, smiling. She rang up my items and told me the price. All was still, well. I looked at the candy and decided to indulge. She repeated the price.

"$5.67."

"Yes, hold on just a moment. I am making a decision," I laughed.

"Make it faster," she replied.

All was not well.

With my candy in hand, I slowly turned toward the cashier.

"What did you say?" I was visibly angry.

"Well, there are two customers behind you so can you hurry up?" She forced a weak smile. I turned and looked at those customers for a moment and then turned back to her. Everything inside of me wanted to defend my place. I was there first. I am still a paying customer and I deserve to be given time to make my decision.

If it hadn't been so hot and my sweet tooth so demanding, I would have voided the sale and left. I felt my anger building inside. I had already sinned with my eyes, but I was holding my tongue. I knew if I let it go, I wouldn't have had a scripture to share. Boy was my tongue jumping to respond! I silently paid. The cashier began being super nice.

"Can I double bag this for you?"

"No, this is fine."

"Well I hope you have a really great day."

I nodded.

I took my bag and sat outside in the heat. I realized that not only did I let someone else control me, but I let my anger get to a place where I knew I could not speak.

While I still have a way to go with managing my emotions I am thankful God gave me the good sense to stop talking. Things in life will make you angry, but it's all in how you handle it. Talking with Michael about it helped me process it so that I can sit here anger free this morning. Confessing it and repenting drops that incident in the sea of God's forgiveness. Now, I must move forward.

We all struggle with something and I don't know what your something is, but remember to pray to ask God to help you through those rough times. He will do it and peace will be just one of the many rewards. Remember, He has already given us everything we need to deal with tough situations. We just need to use what He already gave us.

As for me, I'm taking a hiatus from buying cold drinks. :-) I hope I can recover from that quickly—it's hot outside.

> **Journal:** Have you ever been in a situation where you felt out of control? If so, how did you regain control?

# Letter 28
# Prove Him

*Please read Luke 6:38.*

July 22, 2013

Dear soul,

My father, who is now with the Lord, always encouraged me to give. I've stumbled along the way learning this principle, but I try to be a giver. One doesn't give to receive, but God's universal laws cannot be reversed. Indeed, what you sow you shall reap.

You may think that what you are receiving is not on equal footing with what you give. You may feel forgotten. You may wonder if your journey of growth is worthwhile. You may have so many questions about your life and why things are the way they are. I say hold on.

One thing I know for certain: God sees everything and He has not forgotten you. He knows your works and the intent of your heart. If you are giving to be seen of men, He knows that, too.

The other day His presence manifested in a great way. I love how He asks you to prove Him. I love how He shows up at just the right moment. The other day, I was challenged to be open to whatever He wanted to do in my schedule. I lifted my hands towards Heaven and told Him that I was open to whatever way He wanted to change my schedule.

While I was working on a project, my phone rang. Normally, I don't answer when I am working because it breaks my concentration, but since I'd prayed for God's diversions, I picked up the phone. It was my cousin, Peaches.

"I've got a secret," she said. "Can you come over?"

I thought about how much work I had to do and tried to figure out when I could come over. As I was pondering this, the Spirit reminded me of my prayer that morning.

"I'm on my way," I said.

This was way out of character for me. I am not a spur of the moment kind of woman. I hopped in my car around 8:30 pm and headed for her home. She greeted me in slippers and a nightgown. A satin scarf covered her head and she was holding her dog, Chloe.

We hugged and she led me upstairs to the secret.

Draped across her bed was a large, puffy garment bag. I stopped in the doorway and stared in disbelief.

"Is that a wedding gown?" I asked.

"Yes," she said.

As she began to unzip the bag, I was speechless.

I'd been putting off shopping for one because I am not a shopper when it comes to clothes. Electronics? Yes. Clothes? Nope. Shopping for a gown is the ultimate clothes shopping trip. Besides that, I dreaded the price tags.

"Do you like it?"

I stared at the gown in shock. Staring back at me was the exact gown I'd described to God. Peaches had bought it two years prior for herself and was about to sell it online, but God put it on her heart to ask me first.

It was my pressed down, shaken together and running over gown. It was a reward for striving to be a giver. It was a reminder that He shall supply all of our needs. It was a wedding gift from God himself, delivered by a giver. I cannot even imagine what God has prepared for her!

It was also a reminder of one of the greatest women I've ever known—Mary Wilson, my grandmother. My grandmother was one of the most generous women that ever walked this earth and now I saw her spirit thriving in my cousin. It was a reminder of what my dad always told me: "Robyn, one day the Lord will bring you into a wealthy place."

I am here, daddy.

> **Journal:** Write about a time when God surprised you with something you wanted or needed.

## Letter 29
## A Lesson from Jabez

*Please read I Chronicles 4:10.*

July 30, 2013

Dear soul,

Have you ever prayed this prayer? For years, I didn't. It seemed selfish to ask for more. I am learning that my ideas about life and God's ideas are vastly different. We often sacrifice having a relationship with God for being busy for Him and then wonder why there is so much disconnect between His truth and the way we live.

We are exhausted by self-inflicted stuff and starving for divine connection and perspective, but Jabez got it. When I started focusing on the latter portion of the verse more, I began to get it, too.

And God granted his request.

Thinking more about God and less about myself makes me able to ask God for more. It lets me ask for God's wisdom and presence in the "more." It helps me guide others to do the same.

This week, I asked for more and God has already responded.

And God granted my request.

What do you stand in need of? It's time to open your mouth and ask.

---

**Journal:** Write down the prayer of Jabez and read it out loud today.

# Letter 30
# Judges

*Please read II Corinthians 5:10.*

August 12, 2013

Dear soul,

No one likes to be judged.

It's an uncomfortable situation, really. We live in a time where folks are working hard to blur boundaries that are clear in Heaven. God is not confused, nor will He be mocked. What was true from the foundation of the world is still true. What God put in place cannot be altered, even if we think our voice changes His law.

We set up courts. We make our own laws. We mimic our Creator and think that our decisions are superior—even supreme.

Here is what I have come to know on my journey of hope:

1. God cares about every aspect of our lives.

2. God desires the best for our lives (even if He has to take us through the wilderness first).

3. God is the final judge.

4. We will all stand before Him.

5. He is always right.

Whenever I am discouraged by what I see taking place in this world, I remember these five lessons and they give me hope.

These lessons remind me that even when things look hopeless, I need only turn my gaze toward the Alpha and Omega, the First and the Last, the Beginning and the End to understand that He is in control. He is the Author and Finisher of our faith and the fulfillment of every good and perfect hope we could ever have.

And, even in His endings are abundant beginnings.

**Journal:** What qualities should a fair judge have?

## Letter 31
## Seeds

*Please read Psalm 37:25.*

August 19, 2013

Dear soul,

When you are a child, a lot of things don't make sense.

When I was in grade school, I remember hearing my father read this scripture from the pulpit. I remember him saying it in our home. I remember reading it for myself. As a child, I didn't understand how a seed could even begin to beg for bread.

I knew what a seed was. I'd seen lemon seeds, apple seeds, mustard seeds and grape seeds. To me, they were quite unimpressive, small and odd looking.

Now that I am older, I get it a bit more than I did when I was young.

A seed, though small, is the beginning of something great. From a breathtaking flower to a mighty tree, nothing can grow without the presence of a seed. We are the seed of Almighty God, made children through the acceptance of Jesus' sacrifice. The wisdom of this verse is a reminder that even though hard times will come for the children of God, they will not last.

When it looks like we have been forgotten, we are just steps away from redemption. My hope rests in the knowledge that God will always provide for his children. We need only rest in Him and prove what He said.

Ever seen the tree that results from a mustard seed? It's mighty and majestic just like our God.

Remove your beggar's clothing. The outfit does not suit you.

> **Journal:** What seeds has God sown in your life? What seeds have you planted?

## Letter 32
## Rejoice. Always. Again.

*Please read Philippians 4:4.*

August 25, 2013

Dear soul,

Whenever I see repetition in the Word, I pay attention. Many times, I feel like we need certain things to be repeated so we can really grasp the message. When I look at this scripture three words stand out: Rejoice. Always. Again.

Rejoice - Be glad!
Always - Be glad continually!
Again - Be glad continually, without end!

There are plenty of circumstances that try to take away our joy, but God has given it to us and no one can take it away. We can give it away, but it cannot be taken from us.

When I begin to feel low and beat down by the world, I open my mouth and begin to thank God for everything He has given me, kept from me and has for me. I cannot help but rejoice when I think about His goodness and once I get started it is easy to continue. Stop what you are doing right now and rejoice. Again, I say rejoice!

> **Journal:** Write about something that happened recently that made you rejoice.

## Letter 33
## Don't Grieve the Spirit

*Please read Ephesians 4:30.*

September 2, 2013

Dear soul,

Grief drains. Grief pulls and stretches. Grief ties knots. Can you imagine the grief of the Holy Spirit?

When the Holy Spirit indwells us, He has a front row seat to everything we do, say and think. Can you imagine the pain He feels when we leave Him out of our plans? We try to scale mountains with our bare hands and are perplexed by the difficulty. Meanwhile, the Holy Spirit cries out to guide us and give us tools to fortify our footing.

When we do not allow the Holy Spirit to work on our behalf, He mourns.

I faced several difficult situations this year. After I tried to fix things myself, I stepped back and invited God into those situations. In every situation, the Holy Spirit intervened on my behalf and gave me peace.

I invite you to stop trying to fix things and call upon the Chief Problem Solver. This week, take the time to connect with the Holy Spirit. Ask for His guidance and wisdom. Ask for His comfort. Tell Him you need Him.

Turn His grief into gladness. Yes, I am fully convinced that the Holy Spirit smiles!

**Journal:** Write a letter to the Holy Spirit.

## Letter 34
## Stand Firm in Freedom

*Please read John 17:9 -10.*

September 9, 2013

Dear soul,

Stay on guard.

The evil one wishes to lull you into a jail of legalism. Accept what God says, but sift what man says to separate fact from fiction. Stop second-guessing what God has put in your heart.

You know the truth.

The enemy of our soul exists to sow seeds of doubt, discord and confusion. Reject such falsehoods and embrace the truth of the cross.

This week I was feeling inadequate as a Christian. The enemy watches and knows when to attack. These feelings began to swirl around in my mind that I was a failure in God's eyes. I let that evil voice whisper to me for several days before I recognized who was speaking to me. After all Jesus Christ has done for me, you would think that I would be immune to any other voice, but there I was hanging my head in shame and beating myself up with laws that Jesus already fulfilled.

Oh foolish Robyn! Who is lying to you? The finished work of Jesus Christ was made real in your heart as if you were standing at the foot of the cross next to the Roman soldier. So why would you consider for one moment trading in faith for legalism?

I don't know why I walked that route after 29 years of salvation, but I write about it to warn you today: do not let the enemy guide your Christian walk. He does not know the way. He will send you on a detour if you let him. Thankfully, the spirit is your GPS. He will get you back on track and if you ask Him for guidance and listen to his direction, you won't get lost in the first place.

Be careful what you allow through your eyes and ears. This is a season where the enemy has risen up to steal your hope and change your course.

Stay on hope road, take advantage of the rest stops and refuel when you need to, but keep going.

> **Journal:** How do you protect your eyes and ears from the enemy?

## Letter 35
## Who Touched Me?

*Please read Mark 5:30.*

September 16, 2013

Dear soul,

Sometimes you have to press through the crowd. Jesus hears you, but when He feels you the results are supernatural.

He may not be walking on earth in a physical form anymore, but we can still touch Him. We can still capture His attention for a moment. We do it with our faith. Our faith can become as the hands of a desperate woman reaching for an eternal balm, or a man of short stature who climbed into a Sycamore tree for a better view.

Jesus notices this and responds accordingly. He heals on the spot when no one else can figure out what is wrong with you. He breaks bread under your roof, even though you may be labeled an outcast. He gives life to dead situations and people. He quickens spirits and seals them with a heavenly address.

All you must do is believe and reach.

Get it in your mind that you do not have the answer for your situation, but He does. He is cloaked in power and wisdom. Instead of the phone, the refrigerator door, the pharmacy, or the bottle, reach for Him. Reach Him through your prayers. Reach Him through your actions. Reach Him through your hope.

When Jesus seeks you in a crowd, supernatural things happen.

**Journal:** Have you truly pursued Jesus? Are you trying to touch the hem of His garment?

## Letter 36
## Return to Sender

*Please read I Thessalonians 4:16 -17.*

September 23, 2013

Dear soul,

You are marked with heavenly postage.

When you accept Jesus Christ as your Lord and Savior, your return stamp is applied. You are marked for pickup to be reunited with our Father, who art in heaven.

As the days grow more perilous, I feel a swirling in the atmosphere. Can you feel it? There is a shift in the world of supernatural proportions. Saints groan for the ultimate reunion and enemies of God laugh wickedly as they hurl faster and faster toward an end they hope to escape. Their hope is futile. Our hopes are secure.

No matter what your day may bring, realize that your destination is secure when you are in Christ. Nothing can reroute you from your final destination. You are precious cargo, but remember that there is still room for more packages. Make it a point to tell someone about the salvation that can only come from Jesus today. As I heard one saint put it, He is not coming soon. He is coming right away.

Return to sender. Destination? Glory. Postage paid.

> **Journal:** What do you think about going to Heaven? Write down your thoughts.

# Letter 37
# The Same Power

*Please read Isaiah 41:10.*

October, 1 2013

Dear soul,

Thank God that Heaven doesn't shut down. The Godhead remains in constant agreement—the kind of harmony we should also seek after.

Remember that through it all, Christ's prayers cover you. You are not forgotten. We are His most valued creation and He will not give us over to the whims and schemes of the world system.

Will we be impacted by the way of the world? Absolutely. Will we be consumed by it? Never.

Sure, we can allow ourselves to be swept away by the frenzy of a worldly existence. We can be moved into a house of fear and give up our home of hope, but it is solely our choice. God encourages us to hold up in the fortress He has built inside and around us. By His Spirit, we are protected. By His Spirit, we know peace.

The same power that raised Jesus from the dead resides in us, so shaking boots and quivering hearts are not our signature.

No matter what cards are dealt on this spinning orb, remember who you are and what you have.

You can cause your own shutdown with that kind of power. A shutdown of fear born from the heart of the one who dared to be placed above the Most High. The enemy knows his time is ending. Why do you think so many things are swirling in our atmosphere?

The sad thing is that he is arrogant enough to think he still has a shot to win.

Fear not.

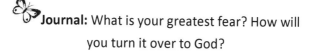**Journal:** What is your greatest fear? How will you turn it over to God?

## Letter 38
## The Lens of Christ

*Please read Psalm 5:12.*

October 7, 2013

Dear soul,

I don't know about you, but I've grown weary of the messages of doom and gloom. Turn on the TV. Doom. Read your email. Gloom. I guess that is why I strive to send a positive word to your inbox.

Don't get me wrong, I don't have on rose-colored glasses, but I choose to look through the lens of Christ.

Jesus did not die so we could walk around with our heads bowed low and scared to live. He came to give us a life we never even dreamed we could have. God wants to bless us. He takes pleasure in cloaking us with His favor. I am a living witness that He is well able to supply every need, even when things look bad.

I will never forget how I asked Him for a specific wedding dress and he gave it to me through my cousin. He used her as a conduit to bless me. Every morning when I wake up, I look at that dress hanging on my door and it keeps me focused, especially when my money runs low.

I am thankful for where I am right now. My income is half of what it used to be, and although my credit has taken a hit, all of my needs have been supplied. I will celebrate one year of being in business for myself later this month and I have a man in my life who pushes me forward. He tells me to stay the course, He says the money will come, but the favor is already here.

When you are tempted to surrender to what the world thinks, remember what God knows.

He will showcase you. Step back and let Him.

> **Journal:** If you had to choose a movie title for your life, what would it be?

## Letter 39
## Wonderfully Made

*Please read Psalm 139:14.*

October 14, 2013

Dear soul,

I was shopping for fruit and vegetables when a small plastic container of blackberries caught my eye. I hadn't planned on buying them, but they looked so good that I placed them in my shopping cart. I caught myself looking at them a lot. I couldn't wait to get home and try them. They looked so perfect! Those tiny purple-black orbs of blackberry flesh were flawless.

I put my groceries away, except for the berries. I took a handful from the container and stared at them in my hand. I admired the contrast of the dark berries against my skin and thanked God for making something so beautiful. I washed them, placed them in a glass container and sat down in my office.

I tasted the first one. It was bitter. I frowned. I tasted a second and a third. Bitter and bitter.

After eating a few, I was tempted to be bitter. I was upset that I paid so much for something that seemed so worthless, but just as I was lamenting over this, God showed me three truths about myself.

I never want to look sweet on the outside, but be sour within.

Jesus paid the highest price for me and saw my value even when I wasn't at my best.

The Father made me fearfully and wonderfully, no matter what is happening on the inside of me at any given moment.

Just by looking at a blackberry, I am reminded not to beat myself up for the shortcomings I have. I remember to give thanks to our Creator for the wonder and beauty He gave to us and to look beyond the outward appearance to find the gem within.

Somewhere tucked in that container, I found a blackberry that was dented on one side. It was unexpectedly sweet.

I will never look at a blackberry (or people) quite the same, ever again.

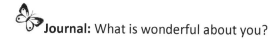
**Journal:** What is wonderful about you?

# Letter 40
# Yes, Jesus Loves You

*Please read Romans 8:38-39.*

October 21, 2013

Dear soul,

Yesterday, I heard a great word. I truly heard.

The word reminded me that nothing can separate me from the love of God—not even myself. The man of God stood calmly in the pulpit and spoke plainly. His words were like fire, and I rejoiced in the blaze.

He spoke about how we can hear a message so often that it no longer impacts us. The fact is that Jesus loves us and His love is unchanging and inseparable. That kind of love is so needed in a temporary, ever-changing world.

Jesus loves you.

Take a moment to repeat that phrase and let it sink in. I did and it was a balm to my heart.

His word is an anchor in a to and fro sea. His word is a lamp to my path. His word fortifies my hope.

> **Journal:** Write about the last sermon you heard that truly impacted your life.

## Letter 41
## Feed Your Hope

*Please read Psalm 127:3-4.*

October 28, 2013

Dear soul,

I do not have any children of my own, but I am blessed by their presence. Today, I wanted to share three small stories about recent encounters with children that continue to feed my hope.

**"Thank you."**

I was walking with my mother at a lake not far from my home. A young boy, no more than nine was running toward us. It was clear to me that he was in training. He had great form and ran with purpose. I figured the least I could do is step to one side to let him pass so he would not have to run around us. Just as he passed us he said, "Thank you."

I cannot tell you how much that warmed my heart. Someone is raising him to be a man of thankfulness and not one of entitlement. This encounter gives me hope.

**"How long?"**

I was walking with my mother, again. I heard the smallest voice say, "How long?" Just then a woman appeared from behind a brick column holding a big-cheeked baby boy on her hip. She turned to answer the owner of the little voice.

"About four years," she said.

The little girl walked quickly along her mother's side. "Is that a long time, mommy?"

"Not really."

"Then, I definitely want to go."

The mother stopped and bent down a little toward her daughter. "Honey, you are in first grade. Let's talk about college when you get to high school."

"Okay, but I want to go."

How wonderful to know that even as a first-grader, this young child aspires to pursue higher education. Hearing this exchange lifts my hope.

**"Did you say dairy-free?"**

I was visiting my youngest nephew's classroom for a program. The teacher was encouraging them to write and had each of them publish their own book. There were visiting parents, excited children and a small collection of hardback books. Each student wrote and illustrated a book and took time to share it with the group. I truly enjoyed hearing all of the stories.

Afterward, we had snacks. My youngest nephew has many allergies, so my sister makes baked goods that he can enjoy. She announced the cookies to the class.

"Hey class, I just wanted to let you all know that I made soy-free, gluten-free, diary-free cookies."

One little boy froze in his seat.

"Wait, did you say dairy-freeeeee?"

My sister nodded. The dancing began. This little boy, who obviously had a dairy allergy, was given new life. He danced to the table. He got his cookies. He brought them back to his desk and talked to them. He took a bite and savored them. He hugged them. He was wrapped up in the simplest of joys—having access to something sweet that would not hurt him.

Seeing his smile strengthens my hope.

Children are indeed a blessing. They are like arrows. How far will our arrows go?

> **Journal:** Do you have children or are there children in your life that you influence? What hopes do you have for them?

## Letter 42
## Do You Have God's Confidence?

*Please read Job 1:8.*

November 4, 2013

Dear soul,

Never forget Job and the lesson his life taught us. God had enough confidence in him to present him to Satan. God knew that, through it all, Job would trust Him.

Can Father God say that about you?

The confidence of God is mind-blowing, but when I bring it down to a finite level I begin to understand the story a little better. Although they are not all-knowing, parents know their children. My mother told me that when she was a little girl, a neighbor accused her of making nasty comments and cursing at her. The neighbor went to her mother and complained. My grandmother listened quietly to the claim. She looked at her daughter and back at the woman and said:

"Naw, she didn't either. Not my child."

My grandmother's assurance crumbled the false accusation of the woman. My mother was vindicated and set free from a jail she never belonged in. The strength of my grandmother's testimony not only dried my mother's tears, but it changed the demeanor of the neighbor. Now when my mother skipped past her house, the neighbor would wave and smile.

I don't know what was going on in that woman's life for her to target a child that way, but I am encouraged by the ending of the story. What started out as evil became good. A parent knows, good or bad, what their child has a passion for.

Maybe God cannot present you to Satan just yet. Perhaps He is still building you up for the encounter. Maybe you are in the midst of a demonic attack right now and you are longing for the hedges to be restored. No matter where you are on your spiritual journey, remember that God is with you. He sees you. He knows you. Trust the process. You will come forth as pure gold and your story will fortify the hope of others.

It only takes one example of hope to turn the world upside down.

> **Journal:** Write about a time when God brought you through a tough trial.

# Letter 43
# Speak Good Seeds

*Please read Proverbs 18:20-21.*

November 11, 2013

Dear soul,

Even though it is one of the smallest members of the body, the tongue has a considerable amount of power—a power to speak life or death.

By His words, light was born and darkness is doomed. The same God whose breath resides in you gave you power in your tongue. You have the potential to speak a harvest or a famine over your life.

So many happenings in life leave us feeling emotionally bankrupt, but we never have to be spiritually famished. When you don't know what to say, say what God has already said. Read His promises aloud and be silent after you speak. Listen for the words that return to your heart; they will be nourishment for a weary soul.

As you continue to be a prisoner of hope, remember the depth of what you say. You are building an atmosphere around you every time you speak. Do not take your words lightly. Plant seeds through your tongue and watch God multiply the harvest.

> **Journal:** Have you ever planted good seeds with your words? What about bad ones?

## Letter 44
## Redemption is Coming

*Please read Genesis 37:23-24.*

November 18, 2013

Dear soul,

What man writes off, God can validate.

Joseph was cloaked in purpose, despite his brothers' attempt to remove it from him. No one can stop God's plan. They stripped him of his glory. They threw him in a desolate place that was devoid of water. Yet, it was full of the promise of God.

Are you in an empty cistern right now?

Take heart, redemption is on the way.

It does not matter that the world has stripped you of your fine garments. They must be removed for God to adorn you with His best. The process of exchanging our earthly dress for eternal adornment is rocky. Stripping must take place. There is no way around it.

An earthly view is so limiting; it is beneath those who sit in heavenly places.

When you are most tempted to fold under the message of man, you must plug in to the Word of God. The Word is oxygen and water to our souls. No wonder we suffocate under the strife of this life when we are far from the true life source.

Whatever difficult news you've received or challenging time you've entered, remember that none of this catches God by surprise. His remedy is already complete. His answers are sure. His peace is a gift. His grace is sufficient. He will showcase you and make it so that you are able to bless others and point a weary world to an everlasting hope in Christ Jesus.

Do not ever, ever, ever relinquish hope.

> **Journal:** Have you ever felt hopeless? Do you know how to restore your sense of hope?

# Letter 45
# Already a Winner!

*Please read Colossians 2:6-8.*

November 25, 2013

Dear soul,

Hollow philosophy echoes throughout the soul. There is no place for it to take root unless you allow it to do so. You can cease to be a prisoner of hope and choose to be a prisoner of deceit. No matter how many ways the world may try to package vain philosophy, the fact remains that man is not God.

As you consider your life, remember that it is Jesus Christ who supplies your every need. Your past, present and future is in His hands. Let His roots keep you firmly planted. Shun the flimsy promises of man. Let Him strengthen your faith so that you can stand firm.

The spiritual forces in this world are real. There is an ongoing war for the souls of men and the mind is the primary battleground. Pay attention to your thoughts, for they are often an indicator of where you are in the battle.

Lift up your head, beautiful soul! Whether on the front line or lagging in the rear, you have everything you need to win. In fact, you already have. By the power of Christ, Satan is defeated. Give thanks for the victory! Rejoice in the hope! Rest in the promise!

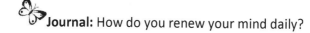
**Journal:** How do you renew your mind daily?

## Letter 46
## Are You Willing?

*Please read Matthew 8:3.*

December 2, 2013

Dear soul,

My fiancé noticed how dirty my car was and offered to wash it for me. The first time he asked, I was busy. The second time he asked, I agreed. He asked me to drive to the car wash. He was already there when I arrived and motioned for me to pull into the bay.

I started to get out of the car because I felt like I needed to help. He asked me to stay in the car. As I sat there watching him scrub the outside of my car, a beautiful truth unfolded in front of me. This is just like Jesus, I thought. He asks us to come so He can cleanse us, but we must be willing. He will do the work, but we must be willing.

I wasn't willing the first time Michael asked to wash my car. I had too much to do (or so I thought). He was patient and asked again. It made me realize that I needed to shift my priorities and take advantage of the blessing he was trying to give to me.

Whether it is a call to salvation, growth or deliverance, Jesus is calling.

We must be willing to come to a Savior who is willing to heal. No doubt that leper jumped for joy as he stood before Jesus in his new skin.

Be willing to hope and know that Jesus will deliver.

**Journal:** What are you willing to do for Christ?

# Letter 47
# Watch Him Work

*Please read II Corinthians 10:17 -18.*

December 8, 2013

Dear soul,

I've become better acquainted with my faith in the past year, but I find that every day I live I know less about what I think I know.

I keep hearing about how I need faith like a mustard seed. Do you know how tiny a mustard seed is? Then, I hear how I need bigger, better faith. Perhaps I've been listening to too many people. Faith is not a formula and has no man-made measuring rod. It does have an originator, Almighty God, and He gives the gift of faith. We play a part in our growth, but we do not manufacture faith. We must learn how to trust Him and step in supernatural places with natural feet.

As I step into supernatural places, I'm reminded that God does not require me to hit a faith benchmark. He just asks me to trust Him so He can show His power in a world that desperately needs to see it, so they may also live by it.

Nothing builds faith like seeing God work on our behalf!

**Journal:** What does faith mean to you?

## Letter 48
## Darkness

*Please read Job 35:10.*

December 16, 2013

Dear soul,

My father used to call night time, "the bewitching hour." I can remember how he loved turning on lights in a dark room. "Turn these lights on," he'd say. "Men love darkness when their deeds are evil. What are you up to?" He'd cut his eye at me and then laugh. He loved light. He used to walk into my bedroom in the morning and sing as he opened all of my curtains. As a child, I'd groan inside and pull the covers over my head. As an adult, I cherish the memory and the lesson; every day is a blessing.

When you are going through a tough time, nights are harder to get through. You don't always sleep well. Sometimes you cannot sleep at all. The stillness can make you feel all alone. Something about seeing the first embers of the sunrise strengthens our hope. It is evidence that we've made it through another night.

Tonight, I pray that you would rest with a song that can only come from our Maker. He is the ultimate musician. His lullabies are unparalleled. He gives us songs in the night season.

Whatever you are going through, remember that you are not going through it alone. No matter how dark the night, the light of Christ is always shining. In His arms, I hear a melody that no one else can produce. Can you hear it?

**Journal:** Do you have a song that helps you in hard times?

## Letter 49
## The True Christmas

*Please read James 1:17.*

December 23, 2013

Dear soul,

This year, I struggled with Christmas. Christmas did not get into a boxing ring and ask me to step up, but an imposter challenged me with folded arms and a devilish grin. You see, there are two Christmases. There is the true Christmas and the distant cousin of Christmas, twice removed.

Everything started out in harmony, remember?

Heaven had great unity until Lucifer wanted God's glory. Things have been a struggle ever since. The battle for souls is real and if you pay attention, you can see a mini war occur every December—a fight to honor Christ or pay the largest retailer.

Is there anything wrong with giving gifts? No. Is there something wrong with making perishable gifts the entire focus of this season? Yes. I was struggling because I could not afford to buy my usual bounty of Christmas gifts this year and I was afraid that it would make those I love feel as if I did not care. After sending my apologies to those I cherish, a wonderful thing happened. I grew up.

I realized that, for many years, my focus has been in the wrong place. I should set my gaze to Bethlehem, not Macy's. God removed the stifling pressures I had placed upon myself. He invited me to sit at His feet and reflect on His perfect gift of love. In just a few days, my mourning turned into singing.

I cried in church as my brother preached about Jesus, the most good and perfect gift that ever was or will be. Because we have received Him, we will never lose Him. He is the perfect size. No need for returns or repairs.

Because we have received such a gift, our business is to share. Not just on Christmas, but every day. He is the gift that keeps on giving. I am glad that our God does not change like a shifting shadow. I may not know where my 1980s Rock Star Barbie is today (that I just had to have), but I know that because of the greatest gift I ever received, one day I'll see my father again.

Priceless.

> **Journal:** Do you feel pressured to buy Christmas gifts? What can you give that cannot be purchased?

# Letter 50
# A New Year

*Please read Romans 12:2.*

December 30, 2013

Dear soul,

We are just days away from a new year, but how close are we to a new life? Will we remain wrapped in the cloak of yesterday or shed our garments to dance like David in the Father's presence?

The world has its ceremonial thought process about what the New Year brings. If we are not careful, we will weigh our existence against human expectations and mistake our lives as lackluster if we are not in Times Square watching a crystal ball drop.

Since we are surrounded by so many messages, both blatant and hidden, it is even more important to seek God daily for mind renewal. A mind that is settled in the peace of God is a sure way to have a happy new year.

As you ponder your plans for 2014, please seek the will of God for your life. His plans are perfect. His plans give you hope. His plans secure your future.

Happy New Year!

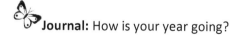
**Journal:** How is your year going?

# Letter 51
# Don't Let Emotions Rule

*Please read Proverbs 15:1.*

January 6, 2014

Dear soul,

I am learning that it does not especially matter if I'm right or wrong on any given issue. What truly matters is how I handle the issue. No matter how justified or unjustified we are in our anger, the response is everything.

I am so thankful that I do not have to handle this on my own. I often forget that the Holy Spirit is standing by waiting to help me in every situation I face. He is there to lace our words with grace, peace and mercy if we let Him.

If you are ashamed of how you've handled something, resolve to no longer live in that shame. Forgive and be forgiven.

Be a prisoner of hope, not your emotions.

> **Journal:** Write a letter forgiving yourself for a situation you could have handled better.

## Letter 52
## All Means All

*Please read Jeremiah 29:13.*

January 13, 2014

Dear soul,

My father used to say, "There is nothing on either side of all. All means all. You are either all in or all out."

His voice echoes to me regularly these days. It's as if all of the things he said to me over the 28 years we were together have finally registered. It's been eight years since my father went home to be with the Lord and it took this long for me to understand some things that puzzled me, then.

I've been guilty of half, when I've clearly been called to "all." That is why this verse stands out to me so much right now. God offers a recipe for closeness, but are we willing to go all out for that relationship? We should be. There is no greater relationship in our lives than the one we have with the Creator. Not seeking after him is like a bird who seeks a lion to repair its broken wing. It just doesn't make sense.

Have you ever torn up the house looking for a remote control when you could just walk right up to the television and turn it on? It takes more energy to look for the remote, doesn't it? I think what drives us to look for the remote is a sense of loss. We cannot rest until we know where it is because knowing makes us feel powerful.

Seeking is natural for us. We have a desire to know and be known. Whether we want to admit it or not, we also like power.

Isn't it interesting that seeking God gives us all we need? When we find God, we understand ourselves. When we understand ourselves, we see our needs. When we see our needs, we understand the source. When we understand the source, our hope is fortified.

Seek God with everything you've got, and then some.

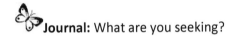
**Journal:** What are you seeking?

# Letter 53
# Justified

*Please read I John 1:7.*

January 20, 2014

Dear soul,

I know it's late, but I couldn't let the day end without sending you a message. If you're up and you are reading this, perhaps this is for you.

Have you ever been accused of something you didn't do? Sometimes it seems like there is no one guiltier than an innocent man. Where were you on the night of January 20th? Or, should I say, where *are* you?

No matter how Satan may try to accuse us, we are already seated in heavenly places. We don't need a receipt to prove our whereabouts. We wear our heavenly address like a designer label. It is by the blood of Jesus that we are justified.

Let the accusations come. The truth will come to light. Hope breaks fetters and loosens shackles.

Case dismissed!

---

**Journal:** Have you ever been wrongfully accused? How did you feel?

## Letter 54
# Able!

*Please read Ephesians 3:20.*

January 27, 2014

Dear soul,

Have you ever read the Word of God and stopped on a word you could not pass? When I look at the word, able, I must stop.

Does it send chills through your body? He is able. You can put anything in His will on the other side of that word. He is able to get you through seemingly impossible situations and ensure that you arrive in better shape than when you first began walking.

As you walk this journey, meditate on the ability of God. He is not limited by our puny roadblocks. Mountains will crumble and seas will part to make way for He who is able.

The next time, you get into a tough situation, close your eyes and say, "He is able."

Watch what happens. Remember the outcome. Share your story to strengthen others.

> **Journal:** What words do you repeat to yourself when times get rough?

## Letter 55
## The Waves of God

*Please read Psalm 93:3.*
*Written with my husband, Michael*

February 3, 2014

Dear soul,

There was a time in my life when I felt as if I had been dropped in an ocean without a boat. It was so vast and wide and tumultuous. I struggled to stay afloat, grabbing onto everything I could find, and when there was nothing concrete to hold on to, I began to sink. At first, it didn't matter that I was sinking. I welcomed the peace as the water pressed against my ears. I wanted to sleep in the midst of the silence. Above me the water still churned, but I was under the chaos.

In my heart, a flash of passion made me open my eyes. I did not want to sink. I wanted to rise above the sea and find my destiny.

I cried out to the Lord and the waters became still. I began to float to the top. I reclined in the water and looked around. I was still in the same ocean, but my eyes could see the truth of where I was. I was in the hands of Almighty God. When I almost let go, He held me up and fortified my grip on life.

Just as I began to relax in the still waters, the ocean began to churn again and sent mighty waves toward me. I felt so small as they approached. All I could do is trust.

The waves pushed me in a new direction. I did not know where I was going, but I decided to trust God. I stopped fighting the water and let it carry me. Soon, I saw a beautiful island in the distance. The waves delivered me to the shore and I saw an angel.

"Fear not," the angel said. "You are exactly where you are supposed to be. There is provision here. There is rest here. No matter what may come, this is where you will stand strong."

When you are at your most hopeless place and feel as if you are drowning, look for the waves of God. They will take you to the next place on your journey. No one gets to Heaven without a rough ride sometimes.

Do not mistake the stormy sea for punishment; look at it as the preamble to the best days of your life.

> **Journal:** Do you believe that you are where you are supposed to be?

## Letter 56
## Lack or Gain?

*Please read Psalm 23:1.*

February 10, 2014

Dear soul,

I mistook a season of gain for a season of lack. I kept saying what I did not have, but kept ignoring what God was providing.

Ever been there?

I decided to meditate on Psalm 23 and take it verse by verse to gain perspective on where I am. The first verse flooded me with a peace I cannot explain. It reminded me that I am not wandering around aimlessly. I have the strength of God's compass guiding me. I also have the assurance of knowing that when I get off course, He will come after me and draw me back into the safety of his presence.

In Him, I have everything I need. I am missing absolutely nothing. I can choose to be stressed about what I think I need to provide and handle or I can realize that God already knows the need and will supply it better than I could ever imagine.

Exchange your vision for His. He has your best interests in mind—not your comfort.

> **Journal:** What is your comfort zone? What do you think will happen if you leave?

## Letter 57
## In His Stillness

*Please read Psalm 23:2.*

February 17, 2014

Dear soul,

God knows the importance of rest, and even though He never gets tired, He gave us a model for rest when our world began. He set aside a day to cease from working and give thanks.

I was talking to a dear lady today about the importance of lying in green pastures.

Green represents health, abundance, newness and provision. We must take the time to rest in the green of His presence. We must learn the importance of this rest.

Father God wants the best for us. He understands the journey and He knows what it will take to get there. Listen to the prompting of the Holy Spirit. Believe that God will carry you through and rest in His care.

In the stillness, He leads and we can hear His voice.

> **Journal:** Find scriptures that talk about stillness and write them down.

## Letter 58
## Spiritual Power Nap

*Please read Psalm 23:3.*

February 24, 2014

Dear soul,

Sometimes you just need a nap.

We all get run down on the journey and need refreshment. When you are weary with the daily commute, discouraged about bills and tired of trying to figure out how to fix your problems, I invite you to remember that the Lord offers refreshment in His presence.

Sometimes the paths we think we should take have not been chosen by our God. We cry out for relief in situations we created and He is still there to rescue us. His name is excellent. His paths are divine.

Take a spiritual nap in the sweet presence of our Father. Close your eyes and rest in Him.

---

**Journal:** Where is your favorite place to rest? How often do you go there?

# Letter 59
# Keep on Walking

*Please read Psalm 23:4.*

March 3, 2014

Dear soul,

Valleys are scary...when you walk alone.

Thankfully, you don't have to. The Great Shepherd, Jesus Christ, guides us over every type of terrain. We just need to keep walking and trusting.

Shadows aren't solid. They are only representative of our fears. You can walk through, over and across them. They cannot fight. They can only appear to be menacing. The trials of this life are real, but held against the light of Christ, they are merely shadows.

When you reflect on this verse, please remember that in all of this, you will walk through the valley. You don't walk to the valley, but through. This means that you have an appointed time to be there. One day you will emerge and stand on the mountain.

When you get there, enjoy the view.

> **Journal:** Write about a time when you felt like you were in the valley. Are you still there?

## Letter 60
## The Lord's Table

*Please read Psalm 23:5.*

March 13, 2014

Dear soul,

When the Lord prepares a table, it cannot be ignored. His place settings draw crowds.

Everyone wants to see what is on the menu—especially enemies. Enemies study those they hate. They are always looking for an attack strategy to weaken those who stand on God's promises. When you are showcased at the Lord's table, your enemies will be silenced.

They cannot stop the destiny Father God has prepared for you. They may slow you down, but they do not have the power to stop you. You can choose to hand over your power, but why? You are seated at a heavenly table, so why would you stoop down to eat scraps from the ground?

Open your eyes to who you are in Christ. There is a never ending anointing in His will. There is everlasting peace in His presence. There is infinite joy in His love.

His provision cannot be beat. Take your rightful seat at His table. Dine with hope.

---

**Journal:** Are there people in your life who try to stop your destiny? Who are they?

# Letter 61
# In the Light of Eternity

*Please read Psalm 23:5.*

March 20, 2014

Dear soul,

We cannot grasp forever because we are creatures of time.

One day, all barriers of time will be removed and we will experience the truth of our eternal nature. Until then, I invite you to let eternity rest on your heart for just a moment. Now, hold that moment up against everything you've endured in this life. I do not suggest that the pain or joy you've experienced is inconsequential, but I submit to you that it is just a fraction of your entire existence.

While we are in the toughest times, it is hard to see the light of eternity, but we live in it whether or not we understand. We are all eternal and will never cease to exist, but our future depends on where we are with Christ.

Have you truly accepted His sacrifice? If so, then why do you subject yourself to the daily defeat He has already rescued you from?

The enemy may be on your trail, but just remember that goodness and mercy are following you every day, too. You don't have to turn around to see them. Trust that they are there and keep moving forward. Just keep putting one foot in front of the other, and when you can't walk, crawl.

> **Journal:** Do you ever feel like you do not have enough time to do the things you desire? Why?

## Letter 62
## An Everlasting Supply

*Please read Philippians 4:19.*

April 7, 2014

Dear soul,

First, it has been two weeks since we last connected. I missed you! I needed a short break so I could return with full strength.

For those of you who don't know, I got married while I was gone and went on a blessed honeymoon. See? I've been busy. :-) Trust me, if you do not hear from me, there is a valid reason.

I decided to share this verse today because I have seen it manifest so strongly in my life—especially in the past year. God has a limitless supply. When I try to place my puny provisions next to His, they do not even begin to compare. I am still recovering financially from a layoff in 2012. I took a hit to my credit and wondered how my score would impact our desire to have a home. Well, let me tell you that God threw my poor credit score out of the window and provided a home!

Yes, as I sit here typing, I am staring at the key to my home. God moved on the hearts of friends and family to open doors and provide for us in miraculous ways. All we did was ask and He keeps showing up in every possible way.

What is my point? Am I bragging? Not at all. I am sharing a bit of my story to let you know that the same God who supplies all of my needs is available to you, too! No matter what you are going through, always remember that you can talk to Father God. Yes, He knows your situation, but He loves hearing from you!

Your pit may be deep, but God's ladder is infinite.

**Journal:** What has God provided for you today?

# Letter 63
# Perfect Vision

*Please read John 1:48.*

April 14, 2014

Dear soul,

Why do we spend our lives as if we are strangers to Christ?

When we go about our everyday lives, He is quietly watching. He knows every part of us, inside and out. I don't even know how many hairs I have on my head, but He does. Thinking about this level of intimacy should bring comfort to your soul when you are enduring unbearable times.

We stand in the midst of crowds visible, but often unseen. It is a rare and beautiful experience to have another person actually "see" you. To see beyond the masks and cloaks we layer so carefully around us suggests a connection with the Almighty. Only those who see know where their sight comes from. Painted smiles and feigned joy cannot stand in the gaze of Jesus and He has given this same kind of vision to His children, but do we use what He has given? Do we see the slow fade of those in our midst?

I am convinced that our trials are like a trip to the divine optometrist. With each hurdle we overcome, our vision gets a little clearer. Suddenly, we see the burdened mother and offer to help her with her children. Miraculously, we see the exhausted caregiver and we step in to provide respite. Humbly, we reach into our pockets to provide financial help to those who are in need because we see the mirror image of ourselves.

Let's all get about the business of seeing as God sees. And, let us understand that He knows what we are going through. You are NEVER alone. He is watching you as you read this line of text. Look up and smile.

Hope brings 20/20 vision.

> **Journal:** Do you see a person in your life that needs help? Is it YOU? What can you do to help? Ask God for guidance.

## Letter 64
## A New Address

*Please read Matthew 28:6.*

April 21, 2014

Dear soul,

I attended a service at the Mt. Moriah Missionary Baptist Church in York, Pennsylvania yesterday. It wasn't the typical Easter service. I didn't spot any Easter suits or frilly dresses. I did see the Lord, high and lifted up.

One by one they came, with their Jesus hats and Kingdom garb; their hands were raised in praise. I added my praise to the throng. We jumped, we sang and we shouted as loud as we could about our risen Lord and Savior, Jesus Christ.

As Pastor Ryan Johnson put it, think of it as the heavenly Super Bowl except we already know who wins.

Since we serve a risen Savior who refused to remain in the wrong place, why do we even consider staying in the wrong place? The grave could not hold him, so why does it hold us? Leave those dead situations alone! Emerge! Rejoice!

When people are looking for you in those old places of depression, guilt, addiction and defeat, make a resolve that they will not find you. When they see that you are no longer in those places, it will give them hope. Your story of victory always helps someone else get free.

He is risen! Let us also rise and be free!

**Journal:** Plan a resurrection celebration. What would it be like? Who would you invite?

# Letter 65
# The Color of Hope

*Please read John 13:8-9.*

April 28, 2014

Dear soul,

I was washing my feet the other day and thought of this verse. You have to get low to wash your feet. While our feet may get dirty, I am certain they are no match for the disciples' feet. Think of the hard terrain, dirt and sand they surely had to walk through.

It is such a beautiful picture of our redemption, all wrapped up in what seemed like a simple foot washing.

Jesus, the Creator of this universe, had to come low to wash us. He knew the harshness of the journey. He knew of the rough terrain, dirt and sand we would have to come through and He was willing to walk that same line. He knew, so He came and washed us with the most unlikely cleansing agent: His blood. Only Jesus can use crimson to produce a pristine saint.

After Peter recognized the depth of what Jesus said, he wanted to throw in his hands and head! Makes sense to me. Clean feet can take you to the right places. Clean hands can help you accomplish the right tasks. Clean minds can produce the right thought life.

Immerse yourself in crimson. It is the color of hope.

> **Journal:** Has anyone ever washed your feet? Have you ever washed anyone's feet?

## Letter 66
## Where Art Thou?

*Please read Genesis 3:9-10.*

May 5, 2014

Dear soul,

In a few days I will stand in a pulpit and remove my fig leaves. I did not seek the assignment to preach. It came to me. To me, it feels less like a sermon and more of a confession. Across my spirit, I heard these words: Where are you?

Like Adam, I've been hiding. What about you?

I know why I weigh 245 pounds, when my ideal weight is 165. I am there because I buried myself in emotional eating. I eat when I am happy and when I am sad. As a result, my temple is suffering. I've been happy and sad simultaneously for the past few years. Thus, the gain. I met the love of my life and lost the woman I knew as my mother at the same time.

She looks like my mother. She sounds like my mother. She feels like my mother. Yet, she is different from the woman I always knew. I didn't even realize I was grieving until today. I am thankful for her presence, but watching these pieces of her crumble has left me weary.

I do not talk about where I am, enough. I try to share it with you in pieces, but I am beginning to understand how God uses our pain for His glory. So, I want to share more and give more in hopes that someone out there will realize they are not alone and there is victory to be had.

Where am I?

Clinging to the only One who can keep us from falling—Jesus Christ, the fulfillment of hope personified.

Now, where are you?

**Journal:** Where are you?

# Letter 67
# Today!

### Please read Luke 23:43.

May 12, 2014

Dear soul,

I love the immediacy of Jesus. He changes conditions on the spot, not after you complete new members' class or receive the right hand of fellowship. In the midst of your pain, confusion, or sickness, He has the power to turn your situation around right now.

Look at the woman with the issue of blood. For twelve years she suffered. No one could help her. Yet, in one moment she was made whole, just by touching the hem of Jesus' garment!

What about the man who was blind from birth? One encounter with Jesus and he was given sight that same day.

Who can forget the woman who was bent over for 18 years? One word from the Lord and her back was straightened.

What about Legion? He went from being possessed by thousands of demons, running around a graveyard naked to being clothed, seated in his right mind.

Even at the cross, Jesus stopped dying long enough to let a forgiven thief know that he was moving to paradise with Him that same day.

Know He has the power to do it now, but understand that if today is not your day, there is a purpose for your situation.

Remain cloaked in hope.

> **Journal:** What do you need God to do in your life today? Immediately?

## Letter 68
## What's in Your Hand?

*Please read Exodus 4:2.*

May 19, 2014

Dear soul,

Everyone has something they can use to make awesome things happen. For Moses, it was a staff. When God's power touched that staff, the Red Sea parted.

What is in your hand? What has He given you to part the figurative Red Sea in your life?

God wants you to be a good steward. This goes far beyond money. You must give an account for everything He has given you. We all have a God-given talent, some people have several.

When you use what God gave you to build His kingdom, your talent turns into a gift. He gave it to you, hoping that you will grow to the point where you will freely give it back to Him. Sometimes, He has to turn up the heat a little to get your attention. He realizes the impact you can have if you will just let Him use what He gave you.

Are you sharing what He gave you?

Are you shy?

Are you deliberately being disobedient?

Only you can answer these questions. Just know that sharing what He gave you will give you a joy you never knew you could have. There is something so uplifting about being in His will. You can shoot up to the heavens when you are doing what He created you to do.

Are you still waiting for something? Perhaps its arrival is tied to your obedience in sharing your gift.

Are you a writer? Write for Him. Are you a singer? Sing for Him. Are you extremely intelligent? Use your mind for Him. Are you fearful of using your gift? Hope in Him.

> **Journal:** What's in your hand? What has God given you to use to make the world better?

# Letter 69
# Remember!

*Please read Luke 22:19.*

May 26, 2014

Dear soul,

Today is Memorial Day. It is a time to remember those who have given the ultimate sacrifice to pay for our freedom. We should never take for granted what we enjoy in America. God has a plan for each of us, no matter how we got here.

As I think of the men and women of the armed forces, I cannot help but think of a man who stands as a General on the battlefield for souls and who continues to direct the troops from a heavenly vantage point.

As we celebrate this day, let us not forget what Christ has done for each of us. Let us take time to have communion in His name and thank Him for fighting for us. Let us honor everyone who fights on our behalf and those who have died in the name of freedom.

> **Journal:** Who do you want to remember today? Who has been instrumental in saving your life?

## Letter 70
## No More Tears

*Please read Revelation 21:4.*

June 2, 2014

Dear soul,

Today is my dad's birthday. He would be 70. Although he went to be with the Lord nine years ago, I still cry sometimes. I know he is doing great; I just miss him.

Crying gives me the earthly release I need to endure. No matter how much of a spiritual being I am, I am still wrapped in flesh and subject to weak moments. I have come to appreciate such moments. They are my declaration of dependence. In my weak moments, God shines all the more.

God is the Great Communicator, so I take comfort in believing that my daddy knows I am doing just fine.

There will come a day for God's children when crying will cease. We will have no need for tears. I'm not sure what your struggle is today, but I just stepped into your inbox for a minute to remind you that the days of loss are quickly vanishing.

Hold on. Ever hope.

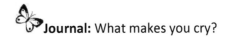
**Journal:** What makes you cry?

# Letter 71
# Abound in Hope

*Please read John 17:10.*

June 9, 2014

Dear soul,

I was watching one of my favorite movies last night and the main character got a chance to talk to his younger self. The actions of the young man would profoundly impact him in his later days. The older man said that it was important for the younger man to start hoping again. The future depended on his hope.

Our future depended on Christ's hope. He believed, no matter what the enemy portrayed, that men and women would come to him for salvation. Even when he was approaching the cross and was overwhelmed by the sin debt He had to pay for us, He stood strong and advanced to the cross to protect our future.

The action of one, saved many.

Who are you destined to save? Who is depending on your hope?

Abound in hope.

> **Journal:** If you could go back and time and talk to yourself, what age would you pick and what would you say?

## Letter 72
## Perpetual Peace

*Please read II Thessalonians 3:16.*

June 16, 2014

Dear soul,

You can choose to be peaceful in any situation.

Easy? Not really, but it does depend on where you are in this journey. I had a tumultuous, emotional week. It helped me to see my spiritual maturity level. There is definitely a lot of room to grow.

When God shows you who you are, believe. If you don't like what you see, adjust.

Choose peace. How? Refuse to be bound by your emotions. Steal away, pray and ask for a reminder of what you've already been given. Peace is in your soul. Let it surround you. Then, when it seems hardest, share what you have.

Someone needs you to point the way to peace today. Model it like a new fashion. The person watching may be you. There is nothing like catching a glimpse of growth in your eyes.

---

**Journal:** Write down the names of three people you can share peace with and contact them so that you may share.

## Letter 73
## One Way to Heaven

*Please read Luke 5:19.*

June 30, 2014

Dear soul,

My sister and I were talking one day about the supposed many paths to heaven. Right then we realized a beautiful fact—there is one way to heaven, but many paths to Jesus. In the bible we see that you can press through a crowd to reach the hem of His garment. You can climb into a tree to catch a glimpse as He is walking by. You can be lowered down through the roof and placed at His feet...

There are many ways to get to HIM, but one way to heaven through Christ Jesus.

Jesus said, "I am the way, the truth, and the life." In a world where truth is constantly being manufactured or bent to suit our selfish desires, the word of God stands without wavering. The fact remains that only Jesus walked the road to Calvary to die for our sins and open the highway to heaven again.

When Adam and Eve fell, the enemy put up detour signs, hoping that no one would find their way back to that glorious place. By His obedience, Jesus not only eliminated those signs, but He also promised a speedy journey when your time comes. He said, "Today, you will be with me in paradise."

He did not say that the journey would be easy, but just as He told his disciples that they would cross over to the other side of the stormy waters, your acceptance of Christ's sacrifice stamps your passport to a place that can be compared to no other.

This world should have an urgency to get to Jesus, much like the man who was lowered through the roof just to be in His presence. Since the world treats Him as a stranger, let us do our part as believers to help them get to know Jesus. If you don't know Him, I invite you to look towards heaven right now and tell Him you are ready to meet.

I hope you know Him today!

> **Journal:** Write down three things you know about Jesus. What does He know about you?

## Letter 74
## He's Looking for YOU!

*Please read Luke 19:10.*

July 7, 2014

Dear soul,

Wrap your mind around this: Jesus came looking for us.

I know you've heard the clichés. God helps those who help themselves. If you take one step first, God will take two. The list is endless, but they are our lists. God came for us when we couldn't take a step. God came to see about us when we couldn't even begin to help ourselves.

He died for us in our unrighteousness and placed His regal cloak around us when we were living far from even the outskirts of Heaven.

He came for you. He came for me. He came for the thief that died right next to Him. He came to a world that thinks "we went." We could not even begin to walk that road to the cross. He did it for us. That was our path, but He walked it in our place. Stop placing so much weight on your shoulders. Open your heart to the truth that He did all of the hard work; He can bear it.

Rest your cares on the only one who fulfills hope—Jesus Christ.

---

**Journal:** Write a letter to Jesus thanking Him for the sacrifice He made for you.

# Letter 75
# He Will Show You

*Please read Genesis 12:1.*

July 14, 2014

Dear soul,

God knows the way to your destiny.

From what I can tell, the place where you belong is never where you think it is. Don't fret when you don't recognize the surroundings. The place of blessing will become familiar, in time.

You may have to travel far from what you know. You may have to leave your comfort zone. You may have to stay where you don't want to stay. It's the price you'll have to pay for walking into your destiny.

Are you willing to take a step? What if everything you are hoping for is on the other side of that step?

**Journal:** Are you ready to take a step?

## Letter 76
## Great Endings!

*Please read Genesis 50:20.*

July 21, 2014

Dear soul,

Sad to say, but there is always someone plotting evil behind the scenes. Aren't you glad God is right there to counter the enemy's every move? Some of the greatest blessings in my life have come in the aftermath of evil intentions.

As you ponder whatever rain or sunshine you are experiencing right now, ask God to reveal His purpose. Those raindrops are there for His glory. That sunshine is proof that your breakthrough will always come.

Hold on! Hope ever!

> **Journal:** Can you remember a time when God rescued you from the evil plans of others?

# Letter 77
# The Tears of Jesus

*Please read John 11:35.*

July 28, 2014

Dear soul,

It may be a short verse, but as I've come to understand, less is more.

I come undone when I read this verse. I imagine salty tears on Jesus' face and instantly I connect with His humanity. Sometimes I get so wrapped up in His deity that I forget His humanity. I forget that He came to walk in my shoes and yours. I forget that he cried because he was moved by the death of Lazarus.

Even though He knew He would raise him up, He connected with us in such a deep way that tears filled His eyes. He did not cry as one without hope, but his heart felt the sharpness of our fleeting existence. He cried because of love.

If you need to cry, you're in excellent company. Let the tears fall, but get ready to wipe them away so you can get a clear view of the resurrection Jesus is bringing into your life!

Come forth!

> **Journal:** Write about how it would feel to see Lazarus raised from the dead.

## Letter 78
## Sabbath

*Please read Hebrews 4:19-10.*

August 4, 2014

Dear soul,

Someone tried to convince me the other day that burnout is spiritual. I can't buy that when I look at this verse. How can I not follow the lead of the Master of all?

Stay away from clichés. If you "burn out for Jesus," how can you be helpful to anyone?

Do not refuse the rest of God. You need recharging so you can carry out His purpose for your life. Even the Energizer Bunny needs a new battery every now and then.

Recharge! Renew! Rest!

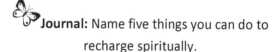
**Journal:** Name five things you can do to recharge spiritually.

## Letter 79
## Overcome with Hope

*Please read John 16:33.*

August 11, 2014

Dear soul,

You have to practice hope—especially in a dark season.

You must surround yourself with hopeful people. You must rest on the Word of God. You must remain determined to stand strong.

Yesterday, I was thinking that you should be most concerned about building your hope muscle when everything is going right in your life. You need that strength for when things get shaky. Things always get shaky. It's just part of our reality, living in a fallen world. Thankfully, our faith doesn't have to get shaky.

My cousin sent me the verse I am sharing today. It reminds me of an even greater reality that dwarfs all circumstances. The last line that jolts me every time: I have overcome the world.

As this world attempts to assault our sense of hope, just remember that this is all temporary. We have a greater life beyond the confines of this world. It gets hard sometimes, but hold on to the peace that God has already given you now and the future He has prepared.

Be overcome with hope.

> **Journal:** What is on your mind today that you want God to know all about?

# Letter 80
# Pleasing in His Sight

*Please read Psalm 19:14.*

August 18, 2014

Dear soul,

We should never be careless with words. Ouch! That cut me pretty deep. I don't always use my words to heal. Sometimes, when I am backed into a corner, I use them to fight.

Am I promoting that you should be timid? Absolutely not, but you know when it's truly time to fight and when you are caught up in a fleshly exchange. Injustice and evil are great reasons to speak out, but getting the last word is unnecessary when you know you're right.

If we would only pause, examine the situation and consider our responses before they roll off of that infamous tongue, we'd surely have less need for apologies. Our words should be blessed by God, not inspired by Lucifer.

Be careful what you speak into the atmosphere. Your response to life's challenges can cause someone to see that there is hope for the human condition. Your words may even help them to remember that hard times will not always be and give them a desire to believe in a new day.

Be a reflection of hope. Speak life.

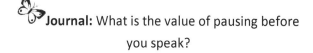

**Journal:** What is the value of pausing before you speak?

## Letter 81
## Access Granted

*Please read Romans 5:2.*

August 25, 2014

Dear soul,

This morning I could not log in to an important account. My access was denied. I kept trying and trying, but the site was down. That made me think about heaven.

It is always available to the children of God. God never says to come back later and try again. He hears you the first time, every time.

We can stand on what Christ performed way back on Calvary, and we boast in the hope of His transaction. I am so glad to know this truth in such a fickle world. We are so smart now that we have become dumb. Fix your mind on Jesus, get on the mainline and tell Him what you want.

> **Journal:** Have you ever needed to talk to someone right away and no one was around? What did you do?

## Letter 82
## The Chief Laborer

*Please read Isaiah 53:5.*

September 1, 2014

Dear soul,

It's Labor Day.

Based on that title, it sounds like we need to work. Not so. It is to be a day of rest and a time to reflect on the sacrifices of the American workforce. I was reading a recent article about the origins of Labor Day and it made me think of our Savior.

I never knew that the holiday was tied to the deaths of Pullman workers who went on strike. According to the article, 30 people were killed fighting for something they believed in.

Our Savior laid down His life for something He believed in. He believed in what we had when we first began. We had such a sweet fellowship with God, and although sin burned the bridge, Jesus stepped in to restore our connection.

Oh, how He loves you and me!

Today, in the midst of your celebration, take time to honor those who gave their lives for better working conditions. Most of all, honor the one who walked the Via de la Rosa to Calvary for YOU.

**Journal:** What belief are you willing to die for?

# Letter 83
# Pray.

*Please read James 5:16.*

September 8, 2014

Dear soul,

Last Monday morning, when I was writing Prisoner of Hope, I had no idea that I'd be in an ambulance that night. When things are going well in life, we may tend to get lazy with prayer. When we get busy, we may forget or whisper a few quick words before we fall asleep. Let me suggest that we are too busy NOT to pray.

There are so many things that can happen in any given minute and we constantly need His touch. Even when things are going well, we should take time to lift up others and ask God for future strength, wisdom, and peace for the approaching storm we cannot see.

As a child of the Most High God, you have a powerful, supernatural link to Heaven through prayer. Do not discount this gift. How many times have you said, "All I can do is pray?" How many times have you heard someone else say those words? Yes, it is ALL you can do and it is the best initial action you can take. Do we sometimes need to put some work behind that prayer? Of course! Pray for that sister who needs a job, but also take a minute to see if there is anything you can do to help.

In all things, follow the leading of the Holy Spirit and watch miracles unfold ushered in by prayer.

**Journal:** Have you experienced a miracle in your life? Describe it.

## Letter 84
## This Same Jesus

*Please read Acts 1:11.*

September 15, 2014

Dear soul,

It took me a while to get my thoughts together today. I just kept thinking about how much the world has changed since I was a little girl. I knew nothing of social media or the World Wide Web. I lived in a time when you had more friends than bullies, Ms. Hazel sold homemade frozen cups for 25 cents from her back door, and you respected authority without question.

While the Ms. Hazels of the world may disappear, and some authority figures bring no honor to their titles, one truth remains constant. Jesus is the same, and He is coming back.

I can hang all of my hopes on Him in an inconsistent world. I hope this reminder brings you peace today.

> **Journal:** How do you feel knowing that Christ will return one day?

## Letter 85
## Keeping it Real

*Please read Psalm 139:2.*

September 22, 2014

Dear soul,

I had a good conversation yesterday, with a beautiful soul. She took on a ministry at her church with gusto, only to be side swiped with criticism. Yet, in the midst of it all, her relationships grew, her spiritual stamina increased, and her eyes were opened.

Sometimes church can be a hard place to attend, but when you go beyond the pew and put your hand to ministry, you really begin to see what Jesus saw. People are a mess. We need guidance. We are inconsistent. We need correction. Most of all, we need love. The fastest way to see the human condition? Start or support a ministry. If you do not grow a heart for people in the process, ask God for help.

To my ministry leaders and supporters, do not get weary in the work you have put your hands to. Have a little talk with Jesus. Ask for help. Seek to have a heart like His. Do not fret when you have negative thoughts—they will come, but they do not have to stay.

And remember that church is for everyone, saved and unsaved. The saved should get stronger, and the unsaved should be compelled to come to Christ. This is all a process!

So, the next time you feel like throwing in the towel, remember these three things:

1. Every Christian does not rest on a cloud and sing hymns all day. We strive for holiness, but we fall short. Give your fellow believer a break, but also love them enough to speak words of truth, in love.

2. Hold on to that towel! Jesus gave it to you!

3. Be the example God called you to be. In the midst of trials, people are watching you. Your life has great meaning. You can either hurt or heal with your words and deeds.

Above all else, keep it real! God already knows your thoughts. He knows where you are. Ask for what you need and He will be your supplier.

> **Journal:** How can you keep it real without causing harm to others?

## Letter 86
## Psalm 139

*Please read Psalm 139.*

September 29, 2014

Dear soul,

I can't leave Psalm 139 alone.

It's the place I go to when I am down. I cannot keep up with all that is happening in my life, but this Psalm makes the world stop so I can catch my breath. It reminds me that God knows me, sees me, planned me, loves me...

**Journal:** How do you feel after reading Psalm 139?

# Letter 87
# Cast Your Cares

*Please read Psalm 55:22.*

October 6, 2014

Dear soul,

When you cast something, you throw it as far away from you as possible. Yesterday at church, a lady asked about my mother's illness.

"What stage of dementia is she in?"

"The-I'm-trusting-the-Lord stage."

I meant that.

You see, I realize that I cannot even begin to handle this disease of the mind, so I chose to cast it on the Lord. He can bear it all. I've had some problems taking my cares to the altar and leaving them there before, but after two years of worry, I let this one go. I cast it away so hard, my arm hurt. :-)

What do you need to cast away today that is interfering with your strength of mind, soul, or body? The Lord asks us to cast all of our cares upon Him. Guess what happens when you comply? You cannot be shaken.

Plant your feet firmly, draw back your hand and throw.

**Journal:** What can you cast away right now?

## Letter 88
## Evil Paperwork?

*Please read Acts 9:1-4.*

October 13, 2014

Dear soul,

The human journey includes miles of paperwork. We have papers that verify who we are. We have papers that track what we do. We have papers that entitle us to property, money, and employment. There are also papers for marriage, divorce, and certifications that we are physically fit and sane.

Satan knows that this is how we operate, so he works the system.

Before Paul's conversion, he was known as Saul. He, like some other misguided folks, thought he was doing righteous work. He even got some paperwork from the high priest to validate his murderous plans against the early Christians. In his eyes, those papers held weight.

In your life, there will be some evil paperwork that is intended for your harm, but God can intervene just like he did with Saul. False lawsuit? God will shield you. Foreclosure? God will guide you. Pink slip? God will provide.

These roads are not easy, but with the Master, you will make it to your destination with a testimony on your lips and a song in your heart.

Trust Him. His Word holds weight.

**Journal:** Has anyone ever used paperwork to accuse you of something you didn't do?

## Letter 89
## Speak No Evil

*Please read Ephesians 4:29.*

October 20, 2014

Dear soul,

At my home church, Youth Share is one of my favorite parts of the service. It's a time when all of the young people at church gather near the altar and an older saint gives them spiritual guidance. I love this time not only for the youth, but also for myself because I always get a great word to help me; we are never too old to learn.

The last Youth Share I heard really helped me. It was about Ephesians 4:29, which instructs us to watch what we say.

When someone is saying negative or degrading things to you, you do not have to respond in kind. There is a fleshly satisfaction in having the last word, but there is no heavenly gain.

God is more impressed when you can hold your tongue and only speak when you have words to uplift. Kind words build up; evil words tear down.

Yes there is hope, and it is fortified every time you choose to look up even when others try to take you down.

Speak well, my friends.

**Journal:** Write down 20 uplifting words.

# Letter 90
# Caregivers, Part I

***Please read Luke 10:38-42.***

November 3, 2014

Dear soul,

I know what you're thinking. Caregivers? Well, quite frankly, yes. Caregivers. The problem is that you may not see yourself as a caregiver, but it all depends on how you define this role.

Let's make it simple. If you provide care, you're a caregiver. Some may provide more care than others, but if you are sacrificing your time to make sure that someone is taken care of, then you my friend are a caregiver.

As we consider these scriptures, we must remember that there is nothing wrong with providing care, but there is everything wrong with being consumed by it. We must take care of ourselves, too. What better way to do this than to sit at the feet of Jesus? He is the ultimate caregiver!

Jesus teaches us the importance of balance in ministry. We cannot be perpetual care dispensers without being constantly filled by God for His purpose. When we try to navigate without His strength, we get frustrated with others. We get weary. We court sadness.

Enough!

Drop your laundry. Turn off the stove. Get out of that long line in the supermarket. Pick up the prescription tomorrow. Stop what you are doing and find a quiet place where you can open the Word of God and sit at His feet again.

Choose the good part. It will not be taken away from you.

> **Journal:** What are some ways you can refresh your spirit when you feel drained?

## Letter 91
## Caregivers, Part II

*Please read Luke 7:44-47.*

November 10, 2014

Dear soul,

As a caregiver, you see or sense a need and you do what you can to provide fulfillment in that situation. We usually don't like to think that Jesus had needs, but His human side needed to be ministered to, as well.

Throughout scripture, we see times when Jesus had to steal away from the crowds and talk to Father God. Indeed, just before His crucifixion He called some disciples to watch and pray with Him.

It occurs to me that, as a caregiver, you seek out and respond to those who need help because you realize just how much you've been helped. The woman in the scripture did not go to Jesus empty-handed. She gathered the best of what she had to offer in the best package she had.

In that Alabaster box was more than ointment; the box held everything that she needed to place at Jesus' feet. She needed atonement. Jesus needed care in the midst of a long journey. She walked away forgiven. He walked away refreshed by her faith.

In the caregiver exchange, there is often give and take. How many times have you tended to someone's needs only to find yourself being ministered to?

Bring your Alabaster box to the Lord.

**Journal:** What's in your Alabaster box?

## Letter 92
## Outcasts, Part I

*Please read Luke 17:14-18.*

November 24, 2014

Dear soul,

Are you the black sheep in your family? Have you been labeled as an outcast? Do you think the sins of your past disqualify you for a beautiful future? Good thing God does not see as man sees. In Luke 5:32, Jesus said that He came for those who weren't right, not those who think they are right.

If we are honest, we all fit in this category because the pain Jesus endured came from our heritage of disobedience. Yet, there are some who have been beat down by negative words from friends and family and feel shackled by their wrongs.

Look up. Make your way to the House of the Lord. You can be free. Cry out to Jesus and be obedient to His instructions.

The people in this passage of scripture were outcasts because of their leprosy, but they heard Jesus was nearby. While Jesus could have healed them right there, He invited them to participate in their breakthrough. He gave them instructions. They complied. They were free from the illness and the label that held them captive for so long.

As I heard Pastor Hugh Bair of Christian Life Church in Baltimore put it, limbs regenerated, skin was cleared, fingers came back that had once been missing. Yes, as the lepers obeyed, great things happened.

Your breakthrough is available! Cry out to Jesus. Do what He instructs. Refuse to be called an outcast. You are included, in the name of Jesus!

Oh, and when you come through as pure gold, don't forget to say thank you! There are extreme blessings tied to thankfulness.

> **Journal:** Write a letter to a loved one that you are thankful for and mail it.

## Letter 93
## Outcasts, Part II

*Please read Joshua 2.*

December 1, 2014

Dear soul,

I love this story! It reminds me that anyone can be used mightily in God's plans. Rahab was considered an outcast by profession. She may have been looked upon with scorn, but I'm glad her eyes were wide open to the Kingdom of God.

She helped men of God. She had enough insight to know they should be protected. She was also wise enough to look out for her and her family's safety in the midst of a tumultuous time.

Her scarlet letter became a scarlet chord and ultimately changed (and saved) her life. Later, through marriage (Matthew 1:5-16), she was tied to the genealogy of Jesus—the Savior of the world! Did she realize what that chord would eventually connect her to? Maybe not, but I am always encouraged by her actions.

Not bad for an ex-prostitute from Jericho, eh?

If you are still being haunted by your past or feel stuck in a current mess, know that Jesus is calling you to a greater purpose. He came for outcasts and from what I've seen, outcasts live hard for Him. They understand what they've been rescued from in a way that makes Heaven stand up.

Cast your hopes on Him.

> **Journal:** Do you ever feel haunted by your past? If so, how can you focus on moving ahead?

## Letter 94
## Outcasts, Part III

*Please read John 18:25-27 and Acts 2:14-36.*

December 8, 2014

Dear soul,

Maybe you don't think of Peter as an outcast, but he truly fit the bill. He followed the most radical leader ever—Jesus Christ. So Peter and the other disciples were not accepted by popular society.

Imagine that. Hanging out with the Creator was not acceptable back then (or now). The Creator! I mean, doesn't that blow your mind that the very one who created the heavens and earth was rejected by the crown jewels (mankind) of His own creation?

And I love Peter, too. He was so passionate. He said what was on his heart, even though his words were often filled with regret. He was a "dive-right-in" kind of guy. He was either with you or without you. No in between.

What I love most about the story of Peter is that even after his denial of Jesus, he was used mightily. It reminds me that God can use anybody. Even me. Even you.

Even us.

Maybe you've denied Christ with your actions or words. Maybe you're thinking you missed your chance for greatness. Not so! God can and will use willing vessels, regardless of their past. Your Pentecost moment will be great in the Kingdom, but you must have open eyes to see. There may not be great crowds and a high podium, but when you stand for God, even in the presence of one person, Heaven rejoices.

Start hoping for your Pentecost moment. It will come.

> **Journal:** If you had an opportunity to speak in front of thousands of people about God what would you say?

## Letter 95
## Fathers, Part I

*Please read Ruth 4:13-17.*

December 15, 2014

Dear soul,

You gotta love Boaz. I think he represents the kind of order and stability a family needs. Things weren't looking too promising for Ruth, but she put her needs aside to serve someone else and ended up with a man's man.

Ruth and Boaz had a son after they were married. They named him Obed. I can only imagine how Boaz raised Obed, but from what I can tell, he raised him up in the Lord. I think his example is evident as you look at his children and grandchildren, and especially his great grandchild, King David.

Were these men perfect? By no means. They all had their issues and struggles, I'm sure. Yet, the common thread of Father God was woven through each of their hearts and it took a father to first thread that needle. Introduce your children to the Master early in their lives.

Fathers can make negative or positive impacts on their children. I pray for the strength and Heavenly guidance of each father that reads this message. Your children and your children's children need you to stand for God in a way that will reach through generations.

If you are standing strong, have hope; your example has not gone unnoticed. If you're feeling weak, have hope, God can fortify your stance. Whether your children are right next to you, living in another home, or even in another state or country, you are essential to their growth.

Take it from Boaz. Stay in the fields and look for opportunities to love greatly.

> **Journal:** Have you shared Jesus with your children or the children of others?

# Letter 96
# Fathers, Part II

*Please read Galatians 4:4.*

December 22, 2014

Dear soul,

Christmas is just three days away. Three is one of my favorite numbers because Christ rose in three days, just as He said he would. As we reflect on Christ's time on earth, let us not forget Father God.

This same Father God is the one who talked to Adam and Eve and enjoyed watching them grow. Sure, Adam and Eve didn't start out as babies in physical form, but as any parent will tell you, no matter how old, or big, or tall, their child is still their baby.

This same Father God is the one who, in the midst of the beginning, saw our end and stepped in to make a change. He exchanged His son's life for ours so that we could be reconnected to Him in a way that we never could establish on our own. You see, religion is about man trying to find God. Relationship is all about God seeking man. God pursues us for a relationship, like any great father would. He helps us learn how to walk and talk, he is patient through our rebellious years, and He is there when we are nearing the end of our brief lives.

Wait! What kind of father would offer his son as a sacrifice? The kind of father who knew that in doing so, his son would reap a harvest of souls, snatched from the depths of the lowest Hell. The kind of father that knew his son would only be temporarily disgraced while men would be forever restored. The kind of father who can turn to his right and see his son at his side and look forward to seeing a number we cannot count arrive in his heavenly abode and fall at his feet.

God is the ultimate father! Let us never forget Him. In Him is our past, present and future.

> **Journal:** What qualities should a good father have?

## Letter 97
## Fathers, Part III

*Please read Genesis 7:12-13.*

December 29, 2014

Dear soul,

As the New Year gets closer, I often think about when the world began. God put seasons, days, and hours in place. He spoke and it was so. I also think of the time when God allowed water to consume the earth. He was very grieved by us, but one father found favor with the Lord.

Because of his obedience, Noah and his family were spared from the great flood. He trusted God and became the best project manager, ever. He constructed a massive vessel able to hold countless animals of every kind, as well as his family.

In your life, you may have to make decisions that are unpopular or misunderstood, but stay the course. When God shows you what to do and where to go, know that even in the midst of second-guessing and opposition, His plan will work out for your good, and your family.

When God shows you the ark you must build—whether it be physical, mental, or spiritual—follow his instructions to the letter and watch how He rescues you and your entire household. Trust Him, and look for the dove. The waters will recede and you will stand on the mountain again!

**Journal:** What ark is God calling you to build?

## Letter 98
## Business Owners, Part I

*Please read Proverbs 31:10-31.*

January 5, 2015

Dear soul,

Nitty gritty. Ever heard that phrase? It gets to the heart of what business owners must tap into to experience success in challenging times. Unfortunately, many businesses fold the same year they open! There are many reasons while folks close up shop, but if you have a business and want it to continue, I humbly direct you to the Word of God.

In this passage, we see a portrait of a woman who among many roles, owned a business. Indeed, from the text, it looks as if she had several businesses. Imports, exports, real estate, agriculture...this woman had her hands in many ventures and disciplines.

Do you have to be the same way? No, but I encourage you to hone in on what you will provide and become a master in your field. From her example in this portion of scripture, we can see that there is an equation for success that involves several components:

**Relationships** - You can't grow a business in a vacuum. Who do you know that can help you? Who can you help? As we help each other, our network grows and so does our reach. This woman couldn't bring food from afar unless she knew some folks who were far away. Expand your circle.

**Communication** - Technology gives us many ways to stay connected, but don't underestimate the power of face to face meetings and outings with existing and potential partners and clients. The woman in this scripture must have been a great communicator because she was well-known and praised. You don't get that from being silent. Open your mouth and connect. Let people know who you are and what you do!

**Cultural Awareness** - Know what people need in your local community and expand beyond your geographic area as your business grows. You think she was selecting wool and flax just because? I believe she identified specific needs and wanted to fill them.

**Servanthood** - In my opinion, some of the best business owners are servants. Look at how the woman in the scripture rose early to provide food for her household. She also worked with eager hands. Eager hands look for ways to innovate and bless.

**Resourcefulness** - Not only did she buy a field, she planted a vineyard on the grounds. It wasn't enough for her to have property, she looked for a way to increase the value of that property. In your business, look for every opportunity to increase value in services, acquisitions, and people. When you invest in the right things, the returns are immeasurable.

Above all, pray for your business and ask God for divine direction. If your business should fold, ask Him to show you why. Everything happens for a reason. Perhaps you needed that venture out of the way so you can focus on what the Lord is calling you to, now.

Dig in to that nitty gritty hope!

> **Journal:** Write down three hobbies you have and brainstorm an idea for a business based on one hobby.

## Letter 99
## Business Owners, Part II

*Please read Proverbs 31: 17-21.*

January 12, 2015

Dear soul,

Does this woman ever stop? No. That is a major key to her prosperity. Should you work at your body's expense depriving yourself of sleep and nourishment regularly? No. You still have to be at your best and honor your temple. Just be intentional in everything (and a few late nights here and there can't hurt either). Keep that lamp on a little longer and press through.

This example shows us that tenacity goes a long way, but so does benevolence. I am sure some of her blessings are tied to her willing spirit to help those in need.

I invite you to spend some real time with these scriptures and ask God to give you a fresh word for your business this year. Still thinking about starting a business? Did God put that in your heart? Well maybe this is your year to jump in. Model your conduct after these scriptures and watch what God can do. He has connections you can't even fathom.

Don't you DARE give up. People need what you have, and they need it now.

Hope you're listening.

**Journal:** Have you ever been tempted to give up on your dreams? If so, what stopped you from giving up?

# Letter 100
# Business Owners, Part III

*Please read Proverbs 31:25-26; 31.*

January 19, 2015

Dear soul,

We know that a successful business takes some serious elbow grease on the part of the owner, but we should also consider character as an essential component to prosperity. Every action you take, every deal you close, and every partner you pursue must all be done with dignity, wisdom and faith.

**Dignity:** You don't have to scrape for *anything*.

As one of my favorite mugs reads: 'You can't do everything, but you can do *anything*.' You must be decisive in what you pursue and be careful not to let your energy be spread across too many endeavors. Know when to delegate. If you find yourself begging for business, reevaluate.

**Wisdom:** Trust God's guidance for *everything*.

Remember, the beginning of wisdom is the fear of the Lord (Psalm 111:10). Look only to Him and His messengers to justify and confirm your business pursuits. If He is with you in a business endeavor, He will not remain silent when you are in need. He will provide a way at the 11th hour to keep you afloat. Trust Him.

**Faith:** Forget religion. Relationship is the *main thing*.

It is not necessary to wear a huge cross around your neck to your business meetings, or greet clients with a Hallelujah. People will sense a difference about you and God will provide an opportunity for you to tell them more. Start and end your business day with prayer, and He will provide everything you need in between.

Finally, let us consider our legacy. Do people know who we are and how we do business? Are we known for honest, fair handling of clients and vendors? Let us strive to be business owners who stand in dignity, deal with wisdom, and are humble in faith.

In short, let our character precede us and we will receive honor when we need it most.

There is hope for your business. Keep going!

> **Journal:** Whether you are in business for yourself or working in a career, what do you think people would say about the way you treat people?

## Letter 101
## Husbands, Part I

*Please read Ephesians 5:21-33.*

January 26, 2015

Dear soul,

I know what you're thinking. Uh oh. What is she going to say about husbands? Look, I am not an authority on husbands. I've only had one for 10 months. Yet, this is on my heart to share, so bear with me.

Husbands, I want to appeal to your hearts. I pray that you would take a moment and close your eyes and pray that God will open your ears to the heart of just one wife who desires to speak for many.

You're still here? Good. Did you pray? Excellent. If you didn't, please know that I took time to pray for you myself.

For the next seven days, do not tell your wife you love her. Don't write her a note about love. Don't sing her a song about love. I ask that you would do something completely radical. I want you to make at least one sacrifice a day and replace something you enjoy doing with something your wife enjoys, wants, or needs.

If you have no idea what she enjoys, wants, or needs, you have a different assignment. I challenge you to spend a week finding out those answers. It's not a guessing game. Talk to her. Watch her. Become a student of her. Get a degree in her. Be able to teach a class on her.

Love her.

An inch of effort goes a long way. Inches become feet. Feet become yards. Yards become miles.

Miles matter.

Jesus walked to Calvary and gave all to show His love. Practice what the Master preached and watch the blessings follow. Put down the remote, the smart phone, the tablet, the newspaper, the hobby—pick up the Word and win her all over again.

Do this and you'll see something beautiful in her eyes... hope.

> **Journal:** Are you willing to change your routine to make someone else's day?

## Letter 102
## Husbands, Part II

*Please read Acts 13:22.*

February 2, 2015

Dear soul,

Can God say that you are a man after His own heart? Do you love what God loves? Do you despise what He despises? Do you wake up every morning and go to bed every night pondering what you can do to please God?

I'm not saying you will be sin free, but if you make it your purpose to chase after what God wants, you can capture not only His heart, but the heart of your wife.

She's worth the chase.

> **Journal:** Would people who know you say you are a person who chases after God?

## Letter 103
## Husbands, Part III

*Please read Proverbs 27:17.*

February 9, 2015

Dear soul,

Speaking for women, I just want to say that we thank God for you! We were created to help you meet your true self. We were created to remind you of your greatness and the glorious calling God has placed upon your life.

Today, I want you to consider who you hang around. If you look at your circle, you should have people that challenge you, can minister to you, and have a genuine love for you. Can you say that?

When you are down, you need someone who can help lift your head. Likewise, you should be able to provide that same kind of help for a brother in need.

Look for your iron friends. You will help each other shine.

**Journal:** Do you have "iron friends?"

# Letter 104
# Wives, Part I

*Please read Genesis 2:18-22.*

February 16, 2015

Dear soul,

The story of creation fascinates me. From the very beginning, God knew how much we would need one another. He formed Eve and presented her to Adam and the concept of marriage was born.

Wives are created to be helpers for their husbands. Ladies, our Adams need us to help them flourish. In helping them, we also bloom. While we cannot force our help upon our husbands, we have the ability to create grand canyons of change in their hearts.

Remember who you were created to be. A beautiful force in nature, not a bystander.

Move that mountain in your husband's way and help shape the world in ways no one else can.

> **Journal:** How can you be a helper? What can you do or say?

## Letter 105
## Wives, Part II

*Please read Proverbs 14:1.*

February 23, 2015

Dear soul,

If you are seeking wisdom, spend some time in the book of Proverbs. As a wife, I have found this book invaluable as I learn to navigate the blessing of marriage. This verse reminds me that I have the power to build or destroy.

I am building.

That doesn't mean I haven't already had to call for help to patch some walls, and I've spent time sweeping up my own rubble. The important thing is, I am aware of my power and I am determined to use it for good.

This week, examine the way you speak to your husband, Consider your actions. Mind what you say. Let kindness be on your lips, regardless of the circumstance. Always take a moment and ask for God's help before you proceed; it makes such a difference.

If you mess up, remember this: practice makes perfect. ;-) Keep at it, and win his heart all over again.

> **Journal:** What are some Things you can do to control your tongue?

# Letter 106
# Wives, Part III

*Please read Ecclesiastes 3:11.*

March 2, 2015

Dear soul,

Timing is everything.

God's timing is perfect.

As a wife, you will find that many people, places and things will compete for your time. Be careful not to get lost in the tornado of expectations. Be careful not to trade your beauty for a painted face.

God sees you. He knows your heart.

Your truest beauty will be manifest in God's time. Hold on.

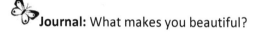**Journal:** What makes you beautiful?

Thank you for taking time to read this book. I certainly hope you journaled along the way. I have provided space here to reflect on and write about your journey. I truly hope this book has been a blessing. I am trusting God to show me how to handle the last book in this trilogy. It will be released in His time. Get a sneak peek of the cover at www.butterflysister.com! Be blessed.

# The Prisoner of Hope Letters

Made in the USA
Lexington, KY
22 October 2017